Ghosts & Legends of Lincolnshire & The Fen Country

Polly Howat

COUNTRYSIDE BOOKS

NEWBURY, BERKSHIRE

First Published 1992
© Polly Howat 1992
Reprinted 1999

COUNTRYSIDE BOOKS
3 Catherine Road,
Newbury, Berkshire

ISBN 1 85306 192 1

Cover painting is from an original
by Colin Doggett

Produced through MRM Associates Ltd., Reading
Typeset by The Midlands Book Typesetting Co., Loughborough
Printed in England by J. W. Arrowsmith Ltd., Bristol

For Dorrie Breeze
– a wise and generous Fenwoman.

Acknowledgements

Special thanks to Mr. Colin Blumeneau; Mr. Norman Pentelow; Mrs. Edna Dedman; Mr. John Snushall; Mr. Kester Bramwell; Mrs. Rita Cuss; Mr. Bunny and Mrs. Nancy Hurst; Mr. Claude Sharp; Mr. Peter Cole; Mr. Brian Foster; Mr. A. Jarvis of Doddington Hall; Mr. W.A. Binns; Mr. G.F. Moss; Mr. Gordon Goodison; Mr. Mark Hodgson; Mr. Andrew Cochrane; Mr. Derek Robinson; Mr. J.G. Speed; Mrs. Dorothy Papworth; Mrs. E. Lyon; Mr. Paul Kemp; Mrs. B.D.B. Wright; Mrs. Barbara Mitchell; Mrs. Olive Cox; Mrs. Annie Wright; Mrs. Lily Peacock; Mrs. Daphne Hill; Mr. Gerald Panter; Mr. John and Mrs. Elsie Lamb; Mr. J. Reid; Miss Michelle Dimaio; Mrs. Jenny Greggs; Mr. P. Birkett; Mr. Robert and Mrs. Valerie Fuller; Chatteris Museum; Wisbech and Fenland Museum; The Folklore Society; Cambridgeshire Community Council; The Isle of Ely Federation of Women's Institutes; Lincolnshire County Council; East Lindsey District Council; Cambridgeshire County Library Service; Lincolnshire County Library Service.

Introduction

THE main aim in writing this book has been to record some of the legends and supernatural occurrences experienced in the old county of Lincolnshire, which now embraces part of South Humberside, and the Fen Country of Cambridgeshire and its borders with Norfolk and Suffolk.

The contents comprise the re-telling and where possible up-dating of established material and the addition of new subjects obtained from the oral tradition, and the overwhelming response to help requested via the local media. Unfortunately a lot was not suited to the format of this book, and I hope all contributors have been thanked and offer my apologies if I have been remiss.

My association with the public and personal follow-up of their relevant contributions has reinforced my belief that there are many strange phenomena which cannot be dismissed as the result of over-active imaginations. Although I cannot guarantee the authenticity of these tales, I hope my discretion will contribute significantly to the ongoing nature of folklore.

Where necessary I have included Ordnance Survey references for easy identification of obscure locations, but these do not imply public access although private property has been noted.

I have also included two small dictionaries of dialect words used within the last circa 150 years, many of which are still in current usage or remembered by elderly people. Hopefully this will add a further dimension of interest to the book, although this ad hoc assortment is purely for enjoyment and has no scholastic intention. Much use has been made of Jabez Good's Lincolnshire dialect book which although undated would, I presume, have been published towards the end of the 19th century or the beginning of the 20th century. 'Lincolnshire Notes & Queries' was also consulted.

I have used 'Fenland Notes & Queries' as a reference for the Fen Country dictionary and drawn upon the dialect section, which relied heavily on the oral tradition, of a booklet entitled 'Interpreting the Fens. People, Places & Dialect', which I wrote under the name of Susan Patterson. This was produced by Cambridgeshire Community Council in 1980, to whom I give thanks for permission to reprint.

Special thanks are also given to the Folklore Society, of which I am a member, for permission to retell the wonderful 'Dead Moon,' 'The Tiddy Mun Without a Name,' 'The Dead Hand,' and 'Yallery Brown' legends. These were originally recorded in Lincolnshire dialect by Mrs. M.C. Balfour and first appeared in the Society's publication 'Folk-Lore' Vol 11, June 1891 under the title 'Legends of the Cars.'

I have been reading some of my stories in a dramatised style to schools and theatre and radio audiences. From their enthusiastic response, I am delighted to discover that live story telling still has a relevant and enjoyable role to play in modern entertainment and hope this book will be equally pleasing.

Polly Howat
Wisbech

THE ANCHOLME VALLEY

The Tiddy Mun Without a Name

THE isolated North Lincolnshire Cars, or wetlands, were drained by Cornelius Vermuyden and his fellow Dutchmen in the 17th century. The Car people hated the 'Dutchies' who were meddling with their land and taking away their living and freedom. They killed lots of the drainers, using the 'Tiddy Mun Without a Name' as their scapegoat, for they knew he would be upset when the water was drained away, and according to this legend told by an old marsh-woman at the end of the last century, he was.

Tiddy Mun lived in the waterholes and he only came out at night, when the mists rose. The creature was no larger than a three year old child yet looked like a little old man with his long tangled white hair and white muzzled beard. He was dressed in grey and laughed like a peewit or 'pyewipe' screech and never had a name.

He was not bad like the boggarts, who were scared of him, or any of the evil things which lived in the wetlands. However, although he was good to humans, and protected them, people were scared when they heard his eerie laughter. When the flood-waters came men, women and children would stand under the first new moon and facing the bog, called out together in scared and quavery voices:

'Tiddy Mun, without a name,
The water's rough!'

The following morning the flood water would have vanished, for Tiddy Mun had taken it away and they knew he would always be their friend so long as the land remained undrained. By now the marshes were almost dry and the water was drawn off into big dykes, so that the soppy, quivering bog was turning into firm land. Everybody said that ill times were coming, but the Dutchmen continued digging and their work progressed.

Then strange things happened . . . The drainers started to vanish and although search parties were ordered they were never found, for Tiddy Mun had taken them and drowned them in the mud holes, where they hadn't drawn off the water!

Replacements were brought in to finish the work and though Tiddy Mun took them one by one, the work continued and soon people knew that the old man was cross with everybody. Children and animals became sick and died, crops failed, the porridge burnt and everything went wrong. At first it was impossible to believe that the little creature would be so mean, so the witches and todlowries were blamed. All the evil ones were punished, but still disaster struck and it was soon obvious that Tiddy Mun was angry with everyone.

Eventually it was agreed that he would only be appeased if some of his water was returned. People of all ages went out under the new moon and met at the dyke edge, each with a pan of water in his hands. As they tipped the water out they called in loud voices for the spell to be undone, then they waited for a sign of recognition.

After a long time the woeful sound of wimpering babies disturbed the unnatural stillness. Mothers claimed it was their dead children begging Tiddy Mun to be kind again, and some said they felt tiny cold embraces as they waited for Tiddy Mun. Then the stillness returned and once more the water was heard lapping at their feet and the dog barking in the farmyard. Eventually the familiar laughter which sounded like the pyewipe screech filled the night air. The spell was broken and they knew that Tiddy Mun was pleased with their offering and pleased with them.

The old people, men and children went home with elated spirits and only the women had sad thoughts of their dead children drifting about in the night air. Soon everything had returned to normal, but for many years thereafter people went to the nearest dyke edge at the time of the new moon and offered water to Tiddy Mun. If anyone forgot, bad luck was with them until they went out and made their customary gift.

BOSTON

A Plague on Adulterers!

IN 1585 much of East Anglia was in the grip of the plague, but due to stringent precautions Boston remained free until August of that year when the first of two outbreaks occurred. During the next twelve months 460 burials were recorded, which amounted to almost one fifth of the town's population.

According to popular lore it was Sarah, the new bride of Thomas Preston, who carried the blame. She was much younger than her rich merchant husband who was apparently unable to satisfy her insatiable lust.

One day Preston had to leave Boston for business at Lynn and having obtained the necessary papers, set sail for Norfolk leaving his wife to sit in her bedroom writing notes to her gentlemen callers. She was startled when a handful of gravel pattered against her window-pane and upon investigation saw a handsome man standing in the garden alongside his chestnut mare.

He called up that he was a friend of a friend who had begged him to call on Mrs Preston. True to her nature Sarah could not resist such a tempting male and wishing to keep her clandestine affairs from her servants lowered a rope from her window whilst the stranger tethered his horse in the stables.

The adulterous couple finally parted at dusk and it was not long before Sarah was in the grip of a raging fever. She raced into town shouting hysterically that the plague had arrived. Soon her death was followed by many others and the dead-cart became an all too familiar sight and sound as it trundled through the streets of Boston piled high with its citizens.

Eventually, the acclaimed physician Williman of Holme, near Huntingdon was consulted and through his pre-scribed practice of disinfecting the homes of the afflicted, the pestilence was halted.

Mr Preston was tied to a horse's tail and whipped twice the length and breadth of the town's boundaries in punishment for his wife's behaviour, which brought such suffering to this Lincolnshire port.

BOURNE AND THE ISLE OF ELY

Hereward the Saxon

HEREWARD is thought to have been born during the late Saxon period at Bourne Hall, which stood close to the castle earthworks. His father was possibly Leofric, Earl of Mercia, one of the most powerful of the English Lords during the reign of Edward the Confessor, and his mother Lady Godiva, famous for helping her husband's oppressed citizens of Coventry.

He was a tall, long haired, wayward youth, with a fearsome temper and eyes of differing colour. At the age of sixteen or seventeen he was the terror of the Fen Country and the leader of an equally wild band of youths.

In despair his father successfully persuaded Edward the Confessor to banish his son from the kingdom. Accompanied by his servant Martin Lightfoot, Hereward set off on the first of many adventures recorded in a number of contemporary and later documents which culminated in Charles Kingsley's fictitious *Hereward the Wake*.

Several years after his banishment he was shipwrecked in a violent storm and washed ashore in Flanders where he married the wealthy and beautiful sorceress Torfrida and acquired his magnificent mare named Swallow who was fleet of foot and was always with him. News was delivered in about 1068 that the Normans were plundering his homeland so he and Martin Lightfoot returned to England, where they learned that on the previous day the French had sacked his dead father's estate and decapitated his brother.

The new Lord of Bourne retaliated by decorating the gateway of the Hall with the heads of several Norman soldiers and the following morning fifty of Leofric's best men offered their services to their young master. Within a few days a full-scale uprising routed the invaders from South Lincolnshire and Hereward was a hero.

More and more disaffected Saxons joined the band of rebels and in about 1069 Hereward's overlord, Abbot Brand of Peterborough bestowed a knighthood upon Hereward at his own request.

He is famous for his success in delaying the Normans capturing Ely and the abbey which was built on an island surrounded by trackless swamps and could only be reached by a secret causeway or by boat through shallow reed beds and shifting mudbanks. The city became the last enclave of freedom to which scores of the disaffected fled.

The Conqueror's men could not find the secret safe route and an account of the king's assault on the Isle of Ely is given in the Magna Britannia:

> 'He caused a bridge or causeway to be made of wood, stone and faggots of all kinds with trees and great pieces of timber fastened underneath with cowhides; but this structure proved so insecure that the greater part of his army in attempting to pass it were drowned in the fens.'

It is thought that the causeway crossed the river Great Ouse in the area of Aldreth High Bridge. Straddling this right of way is the circular earthworks known as Belsar's Hills, thought to be the remains of the castle used by the Normans during the Siege of Ely, Belsar being the general responsible for the causeway.

None of the invaders reached the island and the few survivors returned to the king's court at Brandon for the winter, followed by Hereward in disguise on his horse Swallow. He met a potter who agreed to give him his clothes and wares which enabled Hereward to gain access to the court and learn of the second assault planned on the Isle.

This time the Normans were not only going to build a new and improved causeway, but they were intending to instal a witch in a high tower to cast out any evil Saxon influences. The new construction was fraught with setbacks due to the rebels' interference but the task was eventually completed. The witch sat in her tower muttering her incantations and the soldiers proceeded towards Ely. The rebels waited patiently until they were on the causeway, then set fire to surrounding reeds. The flames soon spread to the new wooden track, killing the witch and most of the men who were either burned to death or drowned in the marshes. The remainder were felled by the insurgents.

Although the monks had plenty of food they eventually grew siege weary and, after certain assurances, disclosed the safe crossing to the enemy. However, one of the brethren, Alwinus the son of Orgar warned the enraged Hereward, who was determined to wreak havoc on the traitors by setting fire to both Ely and the abbey, but was finally dissuaded by the old monk. The gang escaped to Northamptonshire, knowing that for a long time they had held down one of the most powerful armies of the day.

After further uprisings and an attack upon Peterborough, the result of the Abbot's double dealing between Hereward and the Normans, the Saxon outlaw eventually made peace with the king. This was some time between 1073 and 1075 and by now his wife, Torfrida, had taken Holy Orders at Croyland Abbey.

Sadly Hereward's troubles were not over for when he went to court to swear homage to the crown in return for his father's estate, which had long since fallen into enemy hands, the courtiers staged a fight which resulted in his incarceration in Bedford Castle for nearly a year. A hastily formed band of rebels managed to free him whilst he was being transferred to Rockingham castle but Hereward was a reformed man and insisted upon wearing his fetters as a token of his allegiance to the king, with whom he soon made peace and regained his inheritance.

His daring adventures as an outlaw made good tales and even the Normans held him in respect. The French Wake family who inherited his estate claimed to be his descendants, hence his erroneous soubriquet 'Hereward the Wake.'

BURGH-LE-MARSH

The Great Bell of Burgh

IN 1629 the *Mary Rose* left Scotland bound for Plymouth with a cargo of wine. For days the fog had blanketed the sea but Captain Frohock reckoned his ship was close to the Lincolnshire coast. Then the weather changed to fierce wind and rain and the sailors searched for signs of the coastline, well aware that many made a living out of wrecking.

So it was with the inhabitants of Burgh-le-Marsh, which stands on a hill some three miles west of Skegness. They often fired a beacon on Marsh Hill to lure ships into danger and the night in question had all the makings for good pickings. Several people met at the Peacock Inn to discuss the possibility of lighting the fire, but it was decided that such action might be construed as a warning and it was better to leave things to the violent storm.

Being a good christian Sexton Guymer took no part in this debate. Instead he went to St Peter's belfry and gazed up at the big 'Grandsire Bob', his conscience telling him what he should do. Whilst he was meditating his daughter Mary ran to him in great excitement, exclaiming that the ship was about to come to grief and that her father should join the villagers who were setting out for the beach.

Guymer begged her to consider the lives at risk, but Mary left him for her night's work, still urging him to follow. Wearily the old man locked the belfry door and grasped the rope of 'Grandsire Bob', or the Great Bell of Burgh as it was to become known, realising he only had enough strength to toll its warning for one hour.

The assembled crowd heard its great booms thundering over the North Sea and rushed back up the hill to stop the Sexton, and even kill him if necessary. Captain Frohock

14

likewise could not fail to hear its warning. As he steered his ship out of danger he thanked God for his mercy, whilst the furious villagers were still trying to break down the belfry door. At last the shackles gave way, and there was old dead Guymer, his hands still grasping the bell rope, swaying backwards and forwards, ringing the Great Bell of Burgh.

The following spring Captain Frohock returned to Burgh-le-Marsh to thank its people for saving his life. Upon learning the true story he bought an acre of land in Orby Field which he named 'Bell String Acre' and the rent money was used to buy a silken rope for 'Grandsire Bob'. Then he fell in love with Mary Guymer and they were married.

BURWELL

The Great Barn Tragedy

UNDER a large beech tree to the west of Burwell churchyard stands a small tombstone carved with a heart set in a halo of flames, which marks the mass grave of the 78 victims of a disastrous fire which occurred in the village in 1727.

Some strolling players were passing through the village on their way to Sturbridge Fair at Cambridge. On 8th September they hired a barn at Burwell, 4½ miles north west of Newmarket where they performed before a large audience. The Master of Ceremonies kept gate-crashers away by locking the doors securely and then nailing them fast.

Half-way through the performance someone shouted 'fire!' and there was no means of escape. The thatched barn was partly filled with straw and in no time 78 people were killed. Few families in the village had not lost someone in the tragedy.

An ostler named Richard Whitaker was accused of starting the fire. He was employed to feed the puppet master's horses, and climbed into the adjoining hayloft to avoid paying his penny entrance fee and his candle accidentally ignited the straw. Whitaker was tried at the Cambridge Assizes the following March and acquitted of having deliberately caused the fire. He was commended for being the first to raise the alarm, which enabled the actors to escape unharmed.

According to the Cambridge Chronicle of 19th February, 1774, Whitaker is said to have confessed upon his deathbed 'that having an antipathy to the Puppet Show Man was the cause of his committing that diabolical action which was attended with such dreadful consequences.'

CASTLE CARLTON

Sir Hugh and the Dragon

CASTLE CARLTON, which still retains its motte and bailey, is today a small hamlet off the A157 south east of Louth and midway between North and South Reston, approached by an unclassified road. However, according to legend it not only had a mayor, but a dragon!

In the 12th century the countryside was plagued by this beast, who captured and ate the people of Castle Carlton. It had only one eye as large as a pudding bowl and as evil as sin set in the middle of its head and its scales were as strong as the armour which girded its small legs. However, all this did not afford total protection, for the dragon had an 'Achilles heel,' in the form of a small wart which grew on its right thigh. This was protected by a triple guard of brass, as death would surely follow the piercing of this minute spot.

An increasingly desperate Sir Hugh Barde, the owner of the castle, vowed that he would neither eat nor drink until he had killed this fiend which was terrorising his people and presented its head to the king. So he took up his large shield and seven foot sword and set out for the dragon's lair. It was empty, except for a pile of bones and a heap of skulls, the beast itself being several miles from home, digesting two men and a child which had been its dinner.

Sir Hugh tracked the dragon and eventually found him basking with an engorged belly in the warm sun pretending to be asleep. But the cunning creature's eye was ever vigilant. The dragon lay quietly but alert, waiting for its moment to strike. Sir Hugh cried to Saint Guthlac for help, promising the altar at Croyland Abbey many riches if he should win the day.

Then the beast spread its massive wings and flew at Sir Hugh. The knight stood his ground, with his sword at the ready. At that moment the sky became as black as a moonless night, and a mighty downpour of rain fell between himself and the creature. A voice boomed down from on high and commanded him to wait until a bright light from Heaven should momentarily blind the dragon and then to pierce its vulnerable spot.

The voice was followed by a loud clap of thunder and a fork of lightning. Then, silhouetted against the darkness, stood the dragon, with its triple brass thigh guard shining in the brilliant light. Sir Hugh immediately plunged his sword into the wart, whereupon the dragon's terrifying screams could be heard from many miles away.

The wounded creature staggered about in the darkness and finally crashed to the ground. As its life flowed from its body the victor performed his avowed task and decapitated the beast with one swing of his sword. With dragon blood dripping on his shoulders, Sir Hugh carried the head back to his castle, to the cheers of his people who lined his way.

As promised, many precious jewels and sweet smelling spices were placed on the altar of St Guthlac's Abbey at Croyland, and then the gallant knight set off to London and presented his trophy to the monarch who dubbed him 'Sir Hugh Bardolph.' The king granted him 'the right to take a horn of salt from every salt cart passing through his domain and to give permission to all sheriffs, bailiffs and justices to arrest persons within the parish.'

Nor could anyone be arrested without such permission — and the mayor of Castle Carlton was required to go every year to the toll court at Louth to demand freedom from all tolls for the tenants of Sir Hugh Bardolph and his descendants forever. As for the people of Castle Carlton, they were happy to live peacefully and serve their master who had saved them from the marauding dragon.

CHATTERIS

Bricstan's Miracle

BRICSTAN the honest money-lender lived at Chatteris during the reign of King Henry I. One night he dreamed that he was to present himself at the local Benedictine nunnery, where a small portion of its wall remains at South Park Street. Bricstan experienced the dream on several occasions and eventually decided to offer himself for Holy Orders.

His intentions were soon common knowledge and reached the ears of the evil Robert Malart who was at odds with everybody. He would slander Bricstan's good name at the nunnery railings, accusing him of stealing from ordinary people and even the king himself in order to lend money. In his opinion the man was only seeking God to evade the law.

His diatribe prevented Bricstan's entry to the nunnery. Instead he was brought to trial at Huntingdon, where he repeatedly denied the charges and called upon his wife to either vouch for his honesty or condemn him to the will of the court.

She replied, 'Husband, besides what you have declared I have only a few pence and two small rings of gold.'

These were presented, after which Bricstan once more took the oath on the sacred relics. His wife was submitted to the ordeal of hot iron, whereby she clasped a piece of red-hot iron in defence of her truth.

Despite this the prisoner was found guilty and taken to London where he was bound in chains and incarcerated for almost five months in a filthy dungeon where he almost starved to death. The poor misjudged man prayed continuously for help, both to God and to St Benedict, whose rule he wished to follow and he also called upon St Etheldreda, the founder abbess of the monastery at Ely.

One night his prayers were answered. St Benedict and St Etheldreda accompanied by her sister and successor St Sexburga appeared before him, surrounded by a bright light. When they touched his chains they fell to the ground with a great clatter, but the noise awoke the guards who raced to the dungeon where the doors remained locked. They were amazed and furious when they saw Bricstan's broken fetters and puzzled when his fellow prisoners recounted the tale of the saintly visitation.

Word was sent to Queen Matilda who happened to be in the city at that time, telling her of the miracle,

19

whereupon Ralph Basset who had presided over the court at Huntingdon, was immediately sent to the prison to conduct his own investigation. He decreed that a miracle had occurred. Bricstan was a free man.

In time he was invested at St Etheldreda's monastery where his broken chains were hung up as testimony to the miracle and the clemency of St Benedict. Malart, the source of all the trouble was arrested on the charge of heresy and condemned to death. Bricstan lived a long life as a monk at Ely, in perpetual gratitude to the saints who had delivered him from evil.

CRANWELL

Bayard's Leap

ACCORDING to folklore, Meg was a man-eating witch who lived near Cranwell, on the wild and lonely Ancaster Heath, in a cave thought to be a deserted quarry of the famous Ancaster stone. This was located in a wood close to the junction of the A17 Newark road and the B6403 High Dyke or old Roman Ermine Street.

Straddling the car park of the Bayard's Leap Cafe and the adjacent scrub land are two complete sets of horse shoes and one set of studs, each 60 feet apart and representing the leap of a horse named Blind Bayard (pronounced 'Byard') who played a vital role in ridding the old heath of its witch who terrorised the countryside by raising high winds, freak storms and floods. Meg also wreaked havoc upon people, their animals, crops and everyone who challenged or displeased her. Soon the whole countryside lived in fear and it is said that no weapon could wound her and every attempt to withstand her spells had failed.

At last a knight arrived who was bold enough to attempt to kill her. He had the choice of a dozen horses, which he watered at a pond near the witch's cave before undertaking his awesome task. He threw a large stone into the pool, determined to ride the first animal that raised its head as the missile splashed into the water, which was old Blind Bayard. He mounted the horse and set off in search of his prey, considering it providential that the animal had no vision and would not cower at sight of the terrible Meg.

He called at her cave with his sword raised, commanding her to face him. She replied from behind her locked door:

'I'll buckle me shoes an' suckle me cubs,
An' I'll soon be with yer, me laddie!'

And eventually she came out, brandishing cruel ripping claws on her hands and feet, intending to throw herself on the man who dared thwart her.

He kicked Blind Bayard on and galloped towards the woman, swooping down and shearing off her left breast with his sword. Howling and cursing with pain she dodged the second blow and sprang up, trying to unseat her assailant, but missed and ended up securely fixed to Bayard's rump with the talons of her hands and feet dug deep in his flesh. The animal reared up in agony and made his famous 60 ft leaps with Meg still attached and the knight seated firmly in his saddle. He reined Bayard in and turning round gave the witch a third swipe with his weapon which killed her and mortally wounded his horse.

Later that day Meg was buried under a large stone at a crossroads with a stake through her heart and her 'cubs' alongside her. At last people were free to live their lives in peace and the horse's hoof prints (said to have been originally indentations in stones) were carefully preserved in celebration of that joyous occasion.

CROWLAND

The Story of St Guthlac

IN the 7th century, when Guthlac, the son of a Mercian nobleman was 24 years old, he gave up his life of soldiering and joined the monastery at Repton, where he stayed for two years. The monastic life did not fulfil his religious needs and he gained permission from his abbot to become a hermit.

Tatwin the boatman was told to find the most inhospitable and desolate Fenland island and together they set off with Guthlac's servant, Beccelm, destined for Croyland as it was then called. They landed on St Bartholomew's Day, 24th August, AD 699. Tatwin had chosen well, for the tiny island inhabited by a few savage inbred people, loomed discouragingly out of the wetlands.

The trio built three small cells and a simple chapel where Guthlac stayed until his death 15 years later. The site of his cell is marked on the south west of the Abbey ruins. He dressed himself in animal skins and his only food was a piece of barley bread and a cup of muddy water which he took after sunset. He was the inevitable victim of chronic ague and marsh fever, which thrived in that wet and Godforsaken environment.

Perhaps due to these privations he soon became plagued by demons who tested his beliefs to the limits of his endurance.

22

'They were ferocious in appearance, terrible in shape, with great heads, long necks, thin faces, yellow complexions, filthy beards, shaggy ears, wild fore-heads, fierce eyes, foul mouths, horses' teeth, throats vomiting flames, twisted jaws, thick lips, strident voices, singed hair, fat cheeks, pigeon breasts, scabby thighs, knotty knees, crooked legs, swollen ankles, splay feet, spreading mouths, raucous cries.'

They finally carried the hermit off to the gates of hell, but his patron St Bartholomew appeared to him in a vision and gave him a whip with which to beat off these fiends.

Guthlac soon became an established spiritual adviser. One of his visitors was Ethelbald, a pretender to the throne of Mercia, fleeing from his cousin Coelred. Guthlac foretold that Ethelbald would eventually become king and the latter vowed that if this prophesy were true, he would build an abbey on that site in honour of Guthlac. He fulfilled his obligation by laying the foundation stone on St Bartholomew's Day, AD 716, two years after Guthlac's death.

Fishtoft church near Boston is dedicated to St Guthlac and one of its windows shows him holding the whip reputedly given to him by St Bartholomew. There is a legend that as long as the saint holds this whip, Fishtoft will be free of mice.

The Curse of Croyland Abbey

ON Christmas Eve AD 869 the monks of Croyland were said to be indulging in some boisterous celebrations which turned to acts of blasphemy and the abbot Theodore who tried unsuccessfully to check his men sought sanctuary in his apartment.

23

When the debauchery was at its height a clap of thunder shook the building and the devil appeared in a cloud of sulphurous smoke. He told the monks that God had cursed them for their behaviour and warned them that within twelve months the building would be razed and they would follow him to hell.

Time passed and nothing untoward happened until one morning in late July, when a monk who was standing at the top of the central tower looked out across the marshland towards the far-off North Sea and saw small dark specks moving across the horizon.

Their number grew and turned into men dressed in armour which glinted in the blazing sun. A fleet of Viking longboats was speeding over the still waterways and the alarm bell was rung to summon prayers for deliverance before the high altar. As the monks assembled the savage cries of the warriors filled their hearts with terror. The Vikings burst into the nave and slayed the abbot Theodore whilst his brethren fled in vain in all directions. Most were caught and butchered, after which the abbey was looted and burnt. Thus Lucifer's prediction was realised, God's anger was appeased and the curse lifted.

The Danes did in fact plunder the first Croyland Abbey in AD 870 and many of the monks were slaughtered as they and their abbot Theodore celebrated Mass. The invaders opened up tombs in the vain hope of finding hidden treasure. Unsatisfied, they heaped the bodies in a large pile and set fire to them and the monastery before going off to plunder Peterborough Abbey.

Croyland Abbey was to be rebuilt three times and part of the north aisle is used as the parish church. The reputed skull of Abbot Theodore remained in a glass case housed on the north pillar until it was presumed stolen in February, 1982.

DRINSEY NOOK

The Gibbetting of Tom Otter

TOM OTTER'S gibbet stood on the edge of Saxilby Moor in the 19th century, close by the B1190 Doddington road, near Saxilby, known as Tom Otter's Lane.

Thomas Temporel, alias Otter, was a navvy, employed on the Old Swanpool, near Lincoln. He was 28 years old, had a wife and child living at Southwell, Notts and was hung at Lincoln in 1806 for the murder of a young woman, Mary Kirkham, of North Hykeham, to whom he had been bigamously married for just one day.

He had made Mary pregnant and the local authorities, unaware of his marital status, forced the marriage in order that the child would not become chargeable to the parish. The ceremony took place on Sunday, 3rd November, 1805, in the presence of the parish constables.

After the wedding the pair made their way to Lincoln and the next morning Mary's body was found close to the Doddington road with a blood-stained hedgestake lying nearby.

An inquest was held at Saxilby on Tuesday 5th November, and the next day Otter was committed to Lincoln Castle on the charge of murder, confessed and was executed at Lincoln on 14th March, 1806.

It was the custom that criminals condemned to be gibbetted should be measured for their irons before execution, but he was so violent that the blacksmith was unable to perform this task. His body was brought from Lincoln and hung in irons on a gibbet 30 feet high, erected about 100 yards from the place where the body of Mary Kirkham was found, as an example to others.

The crowds came early to see the event and turned it into a festive occasion. Some years later when the jawbones had become sufficiently bare to leave a cavity between them, a willow-biter or blue titmouse built its nest in it. The discovery of nine fledglings gave rise to the following triplet:

There were nine tongues within one head,
The tenth went out to seek for bread,
To feed the living within the dead.'

The gibbet which was weakened by chipping off pieces of wood for tobacco stoppers and other mementoes, was blown down in the spring of 1850, having stood for 44 years. After lying for many years at Saxilby the remains of the post were made into a chair and the head, leg irons and the hook used to gibbet Otter are now on display at Doddington Hall, which is open to the public in season.

EARITH

The Flat Earth Challenge

THE two great parallel drainage channels, the Old Bedford river which was cut in 1630 and the New Bedford in 1650, start at Earith and end at Denver Sluice where they join the river Great Ouse which flows out to the Wash.

During the reign of Queen Victoria a 'Flat-Earther' who used the name 'Parallax' offered a heavy wager to any person who could prove to him that the world was not flat. He was challenged by a man who conducted an experiment on the Old Bedford river at Earith, it being claimed to be the longest stretch of calm water in England. Three vessels were moored, each with their cross-trees at the same level above water. Parallax and his challenger aimed a telescope from one cross-tree to those of the other two, agreeing that if the earth was flat they would be in line. Everyone saw they were not, except for Parallax, who eventually was forced to honour his bet.

ELM

Ignatius the Bell-Ringer

THE old vicarage at Elm, near Wisbech, now known as 'The Shires,' is over 200 years old and is believed to be built on the site of a small religious cell which was once part of the Ely monastery. It is haunted by a monk named Ignatius who died some 750 years ago and over the years there have been many strange tales of people seeing a ghostly figure dressed in a monk's habit, drifting around the vicarage and the village.

Like the present occupiers, the Reverend A. R. Bradshaw and his wife who were resident between 1946 and 1962 also heard footsteps, but Mrs Bradshaw actually saw Ignatius on many occasions and in different parts of the house. He usually appeared at dusk, graduating from a fine outline into the figure of a man, dressed in a well worn habit and sandals, aged about 33 with dark curly hair and thin ascetic features.

She met him soon after their arrival, when the spectre brushed against her in an upstairs corridor, said he was

Ignatius the Bell-Ringer and she should be careful, then disappeared. He materialised on several occasions and finally told his tale.

He was one of ten monks who lived at Elm, which was then a tiny ague-ridden island surrounded by boggy waste land. One of his tasks was to act as watchman and keep a look out for any signs of inundation. Should the waters rise the warning bell was rung to summon people to seek safer ground.

One night he fell asleep instead of attending his duties. A terrible storm caused the nearby sluggish river to burst its banks. Its water mixed with the sea and flooded the area, claiming many lives. Ignatius the irresponsible watchman had neglected his duties and God had denied him a peaceful grave until his crime was mitigated.

The vicar's wife appears to have got on well with the ghost, and one night he saved her life.

She slept apart from her husband and her little dog kept her company at the foot of her bed. One night the animal would not settle, instead it whimpered and ran about in circles, desperately trying to leave the room. Eventually and not without difficulty it settled down, Mrs Bradshaw turned off the light and was soon was fast asleep.

She dreamed that something cold and thin was wrapping itself around her neck and as she awoke from the nightmare, she could feel something thin and tangled lying across her throat, but the room was too dark to see what it was. She clawed away a long tendril of creeper which had broken free from the outside wall and crept in through the open window.

Immediately her bedclothes were pulled away and large hands grabbed hold of her and shook her violently, then flung her across the bed. Her husband snored in the room opposite and the little dog slept undisturbed.

Next a mysterious light moved towards her, out of which came two floating hands which gripped her throat and she could not pull them away. Mrs Bradshaw was convinced that she was going to die when suddenly Ignatius walked out of the darkness and silently wrenched the vicious hands from her body, then vanished.

With barely enough time to catch her breath, the weird light returned, out of which lumbered a man with a huge head and a red face which bore a murderous expression and he proceeded to throttle her. But the dog then awoke and barked as if it were mad. Its mistress managed to free herself and her assailant vanished.

The vicar was still in a deep sleep when his wife burst into his room. He had not heard a thing, but later confessed to newspaper reporters that Mrs Bradshaw had been in a great state of shock, her neck was covered with red marks and her throat was badly bruised.

The frightened woman moved to another bedroom and Ignatius kept away for many weeks, but when he eventually appeared and she questioned the spectre about the creature with the scissors grip, he would only say that it was the spectre of a man who had died in that room. Several months passed before his next visit and he explained that his saving her life had gone a long way towards recompensing for his failure to ring the flood bell. Ignatius was promised some respite from his haunting penance.

The Bradshaws moved to a new living in Hampshire in 1962 but from time to time people still see the ethereal figure of a monk drifting in and out of view, both around the village and the vicarage. One of the present owners frequently hears footsteps pacing up and down above his bedroom at 01.30 GMT, but has not discovered the cause. He says it is probably Ignatius, who has never harmed a soul.

ELY

St Etheldreda the First Abbess of Ely

ETHELDREDA, known also as Audrey, was the founder and abbess of Ely and became the most popular of all the Anglo-Saxon saints. She was one of the several sainted daughters of King Anna of East Anglia and is thought to have spent her childhood at Exning near Newmarket.

In AD 652 she reluctantly married Tondberht, ealdorman of the South Gyrwas, whose dowry included the Isle of Ely. When he died three years later Ethelreda was still a virgin.

For purely political reasons she was then married in AD 660 to Egfrith, the 15 year old king of Northumbria, who was much younger than she, but agreed to her remaining a virgin. Twelve years later he rescinded the agreement and despite his bribes Etheldreda left him and took Holy Orders at a nunnery at Coldingham where her aunt Ebbe was abbess.

Egfrith pursued her and she fled to the Isle of Ely with her two servants, Selbenna and Selvera and Huna the priest. She restored the church reputedly destroyed by Penda, the pagan king of Mercia and in AD 673 founded her double monastery on the site of the present cathedral. She died in AD 679 from a tumour on her neck, which she considered was God's punishment for her wearing necklaces in her youth.

She made a dying request to be buried anonymously alongside her sainted siblings, but 17 years later Sexburga, her sister and successor, ordered her incorrupt remains to be enclosed in a stone monument. Etheldreda's tumour was completely healed and her shroud unstained.

After Etheldreda's death Huna moved to a small island some three miles south-east of March, which is now a slight rise known as Honey Hill (named after Huna), being part of the Roman encampment which lies on private land off the B1098 Chatteris-Upwell road. There he built a small hermitage where he lived for the rest of his life.

When Henry II granted a charter to hold the annual St Ethelreda's or St Audrey's Fair at Ely on the anniversary of her death, pilgrims flocked to purchase laces or ribbons which allegedly had touched her shrine. The Fen dialect turned her name to 'Tawdry,' and Tawdry Laces were cheap fairings made from shoddy material. It was not long before the word became firmly established in the English language to denote anything gaudy, in bad taste and of little value.

EMNETH

The Ghost of Hagbeach Hall

'HAGBEACH' is an attractive private house standing close to the junction of Church Road with Lady's Drove at Emneth and was once the stable block of the now demolished Hagbeach Hall. Long ago this area was haunted by The Mistress of Hagbeach Hall, that is until an unknown stranger stopped and listened to her tale one dark and stormy night.

It happened just as the clock on St Edmund's church struck midnight. The last chime was followed by a blood curdling shriek and the poor traveller came face to face with a female apparition which drifted slowly towards him and begged him to listen to her confession. In between her sobs she told him that this was the anniversary of her dreadful deed which happened 400 years ago and resulted in the death of an innocent man.

Her penance was to walk the route of her crime until she confessed her sins to a mortal.

With reluctance the stranger gave her his attention and learned that the murder happened after the Mistress of Hagbeach had given a magnificent party. There had been plenty of wine and a few of her friends stayed on long after most carriages had left the Hall. A game of cards was suggested and at first the stakes were low, then guineas became hundreds of pounds, then hundreds turned to thousands. The lady had already won £10,000 and, consumed with greed, she staked and lost Hagbeach Hall.

Mad with revenge she vowed to kill the new owner and silently left the room and ordered under pain of death that two of her sturdiest game keepers should accompany her and stalk the man as he walked home. They carried a sharp ended stake some six feet long and waited behind some dense bushes until she commanded them to knock their prey to the ground.

'And as they watched the body fall,
They drove the stake right through his gall.'

The corpse was hidden in the undergrowth and the woman returned home with blood on her hands, which despite repeated washing she was unable to remove. By now her conscience was heavy with remorse and she went to St Edmund's church to pray for the absolution of her sins, her bloody hands staining the pew, the marks defying all scrubbing until the infamous bench was replaced centuries later. Knowing that Holy forgiveness was impossible the contrite woman returned to the hall where she committed suicide by drinking poison.

The man's corpse was found by a shepherd early the following morning, who removed the stake and plunged it into the earth, where it took root and grew into a tree.

This became known as the "Gaul Tree" for it had been pulled from the dead man's gall.

Before she vanished for all time the ghost thanked the man for his kindness in listening to her wretched tale. As for the traveller, we are told he was uncertain whether or not he had been dreaming on that inhospitable night, but 'Gaultree Square' still stands in the heart of Emneth village.

EPWORTH

'Old Jeffrey'

THE Reverend Samuel Wesley and his wife Susanna arrived at Epworth Rectory in 1696. Nineteen years later they encountered a ghost whom they nicknamed 'Old Jeffrey,' and Samuel made several references to it in his journal.

The house was demolished by fire on 9th February, 1709 and it was only by chance that someone saw the figure of their little boy standing at an upstairs window after the house had been supposedly evacuated. The child was rescued by a human ladder and his mother described him as a 'Brand plucked from the burning for a special destiny'. This was John Wesley, the founder of Methodism.

A replacement house, now open to the public, was built on the site and occupied later that year. Therefore when 'Old Jeffrey' came to the disused attic room, now called 'Old Jeffrey's Chamber,' between December 1715 and January 1716 he came to a new house.

It was Emily, the eldest daughter, who thought of the name because an old man of that name had died there.

The family, friends and servants all claimed they saw and heard the spectre, which knocked on the attic walls and floor. Samuel Wesley reported that these sounds became more violent when he was saying family prayers for King George, and when they were omitted the knockings did not occur. Therefore it was assumed that 'Old Jeffrey' was a Jacobite so the rector said three prayers for the Royal family instead of his usual two!

Sometimes the noise of scattering money could be heard, or broken bottles or chairs crashing to the floor and on occasions it sounded as if a carpenter was at work planing wood. Doors in other rooms would suddenly burst open, beds were levitated, trenchers danced on tables and the pet dog became agitated.

One of the girls said the spectre looked like a man in a long white nightgown, whilst her mother claimed it looked more like a headless badger. Robin Brown the manservant believed it was a white rabbit. Yet despite advice to leave, the family refused to move.

The experience of 'Old Jeffrey' appears to have had a lasting affect on John Wesley who wrote, 'With my latest breath will I bear witness against giving up to infidels one great proof of the invisible world, I mean that of witchcraft and apparitions, confirmed by the testimony of all ages.'

EXNING

St Wendred of Exning

ST WENDRED, known also as Wyndred and Wendreda, is an obscure Anglo-Saxon saint who lived at Exning, some 3 miles north west of Newmarket.

Renowned for her healing powers and religious spirituality, she loved animals and had a good knowledge of herbs and medicines. She often used the healing water from her local spring, which became St Wendred's Well, where the pious children of King Anna of East Anglia were baptised.

After the death of her family Wendred moved to the inhospitable island of Merche, or March, in the North Cambridgeshire Fens, where she may have founded a nunnery. Now known as Wendreda, she continued with her ministrations and was consulted by royalty and peasants alike.

When she died she was placed in a jewelled coffin and given a spectacular funeral at March, but in the 10th century her relics were removed by Elsia, abbot of Ely and taken to his own church where they were enshrined in gold. In 1016 the magnificent coffin and its contents were loaned as a mascot to a Saxon army commanded by Edmund Ironside fighting the Danes at Ashingdon in Essex. The Saxons were defeated and the holy relics taken as a trophy to King Canute. When the captured Saxons told him Wendreda's story he became so overwhelmed that he converted to christianity.

He gave the relics to Canterbury where they stayed until circa 1343. They were then returned to March and placed in a shrine which was dismantled during the Reformation and lost forever.

The 14th century church at March famed for its double-hammerbeam angel roof is dedicated to St Wendreda, as is the parish church of Exning, where she is known as Wendred.

FONABY, NR CAISTOR

The Legend of the Sack Stones

THESE well concealed lichen covered stones are on private farmland and permission to view and directions must be obtained from the owner of Fonaby Top.

The Sack Stone was originally one large stone shaped in the form of an open mouthed sack which stood in the north-west corner of the field. There is a legend that Jesus Christ was riding through the fields on His ass when He saw a farmer sowing corn. He asked if a little could be spared to feed His animal, whereupon the farmer, not recognising the Visitor, denied having any grain. Christ replied that He could see a sackful standing in the field, but the farmer laughed and said that it was not a sack of corn, it was a sack of stones! 'Then a stone be it!' replied Jesus and the sack immediately petrified.

Then the farmer's troubles began. The angry farmer found it difficult to plough around this large obstacle and decided to cart it down the hill to his farmyard at Fonaby Bottom. It took some 22 horses to accomplish the task. Then his crops failed and stock died. The man blamed his misfortune on the stone which he had no choice but to return to Fonaby Top. This time the work was done by one horse who easily pulled it back up the steep hill.

It was soon common knowledge that the Sack Stone released its power when it was either touched or moved, although it could be shifted a few inches to accommodate the plough. It is said to have confirmed its powers during the erection of Pelham's Pillar which stands close by. One of the masons chipped off a piece of the infamous stone to incorporate it into the pillar and soon after fell and broke his neck.

Round about 1911 the uncle of the present owner successfully moved the Sack Stone and just before the outbreak of the First World War it broke into three pieces, although this was not equated with that event. These pieces were removed to their present site, although only two remain, one of which is the 'sack mouth'.

Mr Cole has been farming the land for many years and respects the stones which he has never touched. He has instructed his workers to keep themselves and their machinery well clear and small wonder, considering the number of bad stories concerning those who have challenged its sinister power.

GAINSBOROUGH

King Canute

THIS is one of several places in England connected with the famous legend of Canute, the Danish King of England.

The river Trent which flows close by Gainsborough Castle is famous for the 6 ft high wall of water known as the Aegir that rushes upstream with the spring tides. It is said that the king wished to prove to his flatterers the limits of his powers by demonstrating his inability to induce the waves to recede. He stood by the river bank, ordering the tide not to wet him. The Aegir rushed on regardless and drenched Canute who proclaimed, 'Let all the world know that the power of the monarch is in vain . . . no one deserves the name of King but He whose Will the Heavens, Earth and Sea do obey.'

GEDNEY DYKE

Old Mother Nightshade

IN the Middle Ages there was a popular belief in lycanthropy or the power of turning oneself into an animal at will.

Old Mother Nightshade was a lycanthropic witch who supposedly lived at Gedney Dyke in the mid 18th century. The villagers were very scared of her, especially at night and when the moon was full. At that time strange barking came from her hovel, but they knew she did not keep animals, except for two cats which spat at the caged Jackdaw moulting in her front window. All feared the woman, except for a simple youth called John Culpepper who loved Rose Taylor, the most popular girl in the village.

Rose spurned and teased him until eventually his love turned to hatred. He consulted the witch to see if she would punish the girl and was received with pleasure. Mother Nightshade studied her tea leaves and said his troublesome flower could be easily blighted. She gave him a box of sweetmeats with instructions to give them to Rose in two days time when the moon was full. He was then to report back to her when he would learn something to his advantage.

The youth did as he was told and all went to plan. Rose took the sweets without question and being greedy, ate the lot as she walked away. Culpepper raced back to the old woman and begged to know what would happen. She explained that before she told him he had to sit in her chair and keep his eyes closed until told to open them.

John sat down, watched by the two savage cats. First his arms and then his legs were fastened tight and he saw nothing. He waited patiently until a strange voice told him to open his eyes, when all bound tight he had to watch as the hag slowly transformed herself. Her hands, her arms, her legs and torso and finally her face, with gnashing teeth in a drooling mouth, all covered in thick brown hair.

That night the villagers stayed locked in their homes, trembling at the sound of savage growls and cries for help coming from Mother Nightshade's cottage. A group of brave men called on the woman at dawn, but she was not at home. However, there was a large pile of John Culpepper's blood-stained clothes thrown into a dark corner, together with a heap of bones. The boy was never seen again, but the beautiful Rose flourished with never a thought for the gullible boy who had loved her.

The parson was summoned to the scene of the crime but refused his assistance. So they set fire to the hovel and although the witch was never seen again, the eerie barking continued under the full moon. The people from Gedney Dyke never left their homes then.

GOREFIELD

Scrimshaw's Poltergeist

IN 1909 Joe Scrimshaw, the fruit farmer had a new house built on the old Turnover Bank, which soon became known as 'The Haunted House.'

Sometime between moving in and the start of the haunting, which was on the 12th February, 1923, his wife had left him taking one of their two children with her. The other, Olive, who was 14 years old when the happening occurred, lived with Skrimmie and his mother who received help from a daily woman named Harriet Ward.

Strange things happened in the late afternoon when Granny Scrimshaw tried without success to light the oil lamps and had to send Olive out to borrow candles from a neighbour. They too refused to be lit, neither would they flare for Joe who ate his supper in a bad mood.

Suddenly, in the half light of the sitting room fire which was struggling to keep alight, the Angelus Pianola which was estimated to weigh some five hundredweight, slid by itself from its place against the wall and moved about the room, then toppled in a jangling heap on the floor.

This was followed by the pictures dropping one by one from the wall, ornaments falling from the mantelpiece and the heavy dining table scuttling about like the pianola. Worse was to come when the barometer, Joe's most valued possession, leaped down onto the floor to join the picture glass and figurines.

Then crashing came from the kitchen and so to avoid more damage, the crockery was stacked neatly on the large table instead of balanced in the china pantry. The door was locked and a few minutes later everything was dashed to smithereens on the floor. Nothing was chipped or cracked in two, everything was reduced to shards.

Neighbours were called in and witnessed the mayhem and after a night of further uproar Olive was sent to lodge with relatives in Norfolk and never returned to live in her father's house.

Word soon got out that Skrimmie had a poltergeist and this attracted the local and national press plus lots of sightseers who got the rough edge of Joe's sharp tongue. He also received a lot of letters which included one from Sir Arthur Conan Doyle who thought his teenage daughter could have encouraged the poltergeist. He suggested amongst other things that the house should be well ventilated, but the troubles remained even with fresh air and Olive's absence.

The local vicar was not interested in Joe's predicament, but a farmer from neighbouring Wisbech St Mary was. He suggested that perhaps he had not got a poltergeist, maybe someone had cast the Evil Eye upon him. He suggested that Harriet Mary Holmes, the local wise-woman cum smallholder, of Chalk Road, might be able to exorcise the place and I am told the *News of the World* paid her fee. She went to the lonely house on Turnover Bank where she performed her traditional spell-breaking, using a small medicine bottle filled with a number of black-headed apple pips, some pins, a paring from Joe's fingernail and pieces of hair taken from his mother and daughter. The bottle was well stoppered and placed in the hot coals of the kitchen range, then she locked the door and would not let the Scrimshaws in until the bottle had burst from the heat of the fire, taking the hex with it.

The spell-breaker was quite commonplace, using intimate links with the possessed and the malevolence, but did it really work or was 'it,' albeit the Evil Eye or the Poltergeist, more clever than the wise-woman? For on 6th March Mrs Holmes was found face down, drowned in some six inches of dyke water. Everybody agreed that the old lady, who was in robust health and knew the area like the back of her hand, had no business being in the dyke.

She lies in Gorefield churchyard beside her husband John, but the strange thing is, that just about the time of her death, Joe Scrimshaw reckoned all hell broke loose in his house for just a few minutes, then 'it' went away. Although never again aware of the presence, others have been and are!

GRIMSBY

Havelock the Dane

ALTHOUGH there are many versions of the following legend, they all agree that Grim founded the town of Grimsby and that Havelock granted it many immunities when he became king.

Over a thousand years ago, when the popular English king Athelwold was on the point of death, he appointed Earl Godrich of Cornwall as his regent and guardian of his infant child Goldborough who was to inherit the throne when she was 21 years old and be married to the best and strongest man alive. The earl affirmed all this on the Bible and after the king's death claimed the whole of England.

Goldborough grew into a beautiful, gentle young woman, but Godrich was jealous of her and sent her to Dover, where she was kept in poverty and isolation.

At the time of Athewold's death, the good king Birkabeyn of Denmark was also dying. He arranged for his friend Carl Godard to be his regent and guardian of his two daughters and one son named Havelock, who was to inherit the throne when he reached the age of majority. Godard swore his loyalty on the Bible, but when the king died took the boy and his sisters Swanborough and Helfled and imprisoned them in a castle.

The children were kept hungry and eventually he took the two girls and slit their throats. Havelock was to be thrown into the sea and Grim the fisherman was to do the deed that night in return for great riches and freedom from slavery. Godard would accept the blame.

Unaware of his true identity, Grim bound and gagged the boy, but on the point of drowning saw a shining light around the child and a ray like a sunbeam which came from his mouth. He untied his bonds and discovered a bright king-mark on his right shoulder.

He knew his prisoner was the Danish heir and fell at his feet. Havelock forgave him in return for his life. The following morning he went to Godard, claiming the deed had been done and demanding his freedom. The villain denied all knowledge of the bargain and threatened the fisherman with death. The frightened man took Havelock, his wife and three sons to his boat and sailed from Denmark but a strong wind blew from the north driving them to England. They landed in the Humber, at the northern end of Lindsey where they built a house of earth and because Grim owned the place it was named Grimsby.

He was a skilful fisherman and he, his sons and Havelock worked hard, but in time their fortunes changed and they were starving. Grim begged the Dane to go to Lincoln where he could find a little food for himself and made a cloak from his sail to keep the boy dry.

Half naked and without shoes, Havelock walked to Lincoln and took work as a scullion. The boy grew into a tall, strong young man and looked every part a king.

At that time Earl Godrich held a parliament at Lincoln and the occasion was celebrated by a games tournament, of which Havelock became the champion. All the knights at the castle spoke of the scullion's strength and good

43

looks, which made Godrich remember his promise to marry Athelwold's daughter to the fairest and strongest man. He decided that the kitchen hand should have the princess Goldborough and ordered her to be brought to Lincoln. She announced that she would marry none other than a king and Havelock refused marriage, but Godrich threatened them with torture and death and so the two were wed, neither divulging their true identity.

Having nowhere to live they set out for Grimsby where they learned that Grim was dead, but his now prosperous sons offered them to share their home. That night when she lay beside her husband, Goldborough saw a shining light from Havelock's mouth and a cross of red gold on his shoulder. Then an angel told her that the cross was a token that Havelock was the heir of a king and would rule all Denmark and England and she would be queen.

The next morning Havelock related strange dreams. He sat on a high hill in Denmark and as he sat there he began to own the whole country and he held that country in his arms and its people loved him. Then he had another dream. He flew over the sea and came to England and held it in his hand and gave it to Goldborough.

In time, with the help of Grim's three brave sons, the earl Godrich and Carl Godard were punished and Havelock and Goldborough ruled both countries with justice and kindness for 60 years and had 15 children.

HOLBEACH

The Holbeach Gamesters

FOR many years during the 17th century Abraham Tegerdine, Mr Slater, Dr Jonathan Watson and Farmer Guymer who were the town's notorious young gamesters, met at the Chequers Inn where they gambled and drank until the farmer's death spoilt things.

They were at their favourite inn, which still stands in the centre of the town, on the eve of the burial, lamenting the passing of their good times, for no one could replace that sporting farmer. The men became more and more maudlin, until Abraham Tegerdine suggested they should go over to the church and keep their dead friend company.

With true drunkards' courage, they pocketed their cards, ordered more beer and a lamp, and staggered over the road to All Saints Church. They opened the door with difficulty and slewed their way up the aisle to the altar steps where they offered their silent friend several toasts. Time dragged as they kept watch in the cold church, until Tegerdine suggested a game of cards and they used the coffin lid for a table.

The cards were dealt, but of course they were a man short. It was Tegerdine's suggestion that the corpse would make an excellent dummy, and so the lid was prised open and Guymer pulled out and propped up alongside his old friends. They took turns to play the dummy's cards and the beer flowed. The corpse was congratulated for playing so well, indeed much better than when alive and kicking at the Chequers!

Suddenly the dead man turned his head and leering at the gamesters, summoned three demons to spirit away forever the now screaming Slater, Watson and Tegerdine.

At sunrise the townspeople, who had heard the rumpus in the night, now dared to enter the church, where they discovered the upturned coffin and a deck of cards scattered on the floor. Seated against the altar rails was the body of farmer Guymer with a smug, self satisfied look on his putty-coloured face. It is said that for many years thereafter four men could be plainly seen standing by the church, beckoning all drunkards to their fate.

HOLYWELL

The Ghost of the Ferry Boat Inn

THE inn is best approached from Church Street and past St John the Baptist's church, with its holy well which is dressed during the annual church festival held in June.

Each year on the 17th March the village, which lies south east of Huntingdon and next to the river Great Ouse, is invaded by crowds of people making their way to the Ferry Boat Inn. They jostle together in the bar at midnight in the hope of seeing the spectre of Juliet Tewsley arise from her grave set in the floor of the bar. She is said to have been spurned by Thomas Zoul the woodcutter, and hanged herself from a tree by the river on the 17th March, 1050.

Juliet fell in love as he passed her one early spring morning when she was picking flowers in the wood. Zoul did not notice her then or when she hid behind a tree each day to watch him stride out for work. Finally this shy girl had to declare her love and offered him flowers, which he threw to the ground. She lay on the ground and wept beside the scattered blooms until nightfall, when she took a length of rope from a farmer's barn and hanged herself from a tree.

The authorities ruled that Juliet should be interred at the crossroads, being the usual place for those who committed suicide. Eighteen years later the Ferry Boat Inn was built close to her grave which was marked with a single stone slab. In time the inn was extended and Juliet's stone was left to form part of the floor, where it remains uncarpeted and out of which Juliet has allegedly been seen to arise on the anniversary of her death.

ISLE OF AXEHOLME

The Dead Moon

BEFORE the Isle was drained in the 17th century, it was full of pools of black water, and squelching wetlands. Many marsh people met with watery graves on moonless nights when they could not see the paths clearly and stories grew that they were lured to their fate by all the things which lived in the darkness, doing evil to those who were not safely beside their firesides: will o' the wisps, bogles, dead things, witches and crawling horrors.

A legend of this time concerns the moon who got to hear about these evils of the wetlands when her back was turned and the nights were darkest. At the month end, the story goes, she came to earth in a black cloak with a hood pulled over her yellow shining hair. She went to the bog edge and looked about her, and then walked right into the middle of the bogs. And what a sight met her eyes! Witches rode past on great broomsticks, the evil eye glowered from the darkest corners and the will o' the wisps danced about with their lanterns swinging on their backs. Then the dead folk rose in the water, their slimy dead hands beckoning and pointing to the deep pools.

The moon trembled and drew her cloak fast about her, but was determined to see everything. Just as she came upon a big black pool, her foot slipped. She managed to grab with both hands at a snag nearby, but it wound itself around her hands and gripped her so that she could not move.

As she pulled and twisted to free herself she heard a voice which repeatedly called then died away with a sob, until the marshes were full of the pitiful crying sound. Then she heard footsteps floundering along and finally a terrified white face.

It was a man who had strayed into the bogs, and round about him the grinning bogles and the dead folk and the creeping horrors crawled and cried, their voices mocking him and the dead hands plucking him, and ahead the will o' the wisps dangled their lanterns and shook with evil glee as they led him further and further from the safe track.

Half-crazy with fear he struggled on towards the flickering lights which looked like help and safety. When the moon saw that the man was coming nearer and nearer to the deep holes and straying further and further from the path, she struggled and pulled again at the snag, which held her fast. All the twisting pulled the black hood from her shining hair and its radiance shone in the darkness and drove the evil things back into their dark corners.

Rejoicing at his escape, the traveller fled from the bog-lands as fast as he could to the safety of the path. But the moon was still imprisoned and needed help herself. Her head dropped with sadness and the hood once more covered her light. Back came the darkness and with it the evil things which crowded and mocked her, shrieking with rage and spite, swearing, spitting and snarling.

Now that she was in their power, the creatures fought and squabbled all the rest of the night over what they should do with her. Then the dawn light streaked across the sky. They knew they had to act quickly and so they pushed her deep in the water at the foot of the snag. The dead folk held her down, while the bogles found a big stone and rolled it on top of her, to keep her from rising.

Days went by. It was time for the new moon, but the moon did not shine. One night, when the men were talking in the inn about the lost moon, a stranger from the far end of the bog-lands heard their conversation. He told them of his ordeal in the bog and how the miraculous light drove away the evil things and showed him the right track across the marshes. He told them it came from something standing in a black snag in the water. He recalled seeing a shining face and yellow hair like the full moon herself about the marshes at night.

They consulted the local wise woman, who told them to search that night for a place in the bog where they would find a coffin, a candle and a cross and there they would find the moon.

So as dusk fell they set out together, along the dark paths to the middle of the bogs searching all the time for the coffin, the candle and the cross, until at last they came to the pool by the side of the Great Snag.

There was the huge stone, half in and half out of the water, looking like a strange big coffin. At its head the snag stretched its two arms in a dark gruesome cross and on it a light flickered, like a tiny candle. The men knelt down in the wet, crossed themselves and silently recited the Lord's prayer, first forwards because of the cross and then backwards to keep off the bogles.

When this was accomplished, the stone was removed and for one moment the men saw a strange and beautiful face looking up out of the black water before its brilliance

49

dazzled them. As soon as the marsh men had regained their sight, the moon was back in the sky illuminating the darkness once more.

From that time, it is said, the moon shone even more brightly over the wet-lands, for she had experienced herself the horrors of the darkness.

LEVERINGTON

A Devillish Whirling

ONE day a widow was baking cakes to celebrate Mid-Lent or Mothering Sunday. She was removing a batch from the oven when the devil appeared in a whirlwind which blew through her kitchen door. He snatched her up in his arms and together they flew right over the church, to the horror of the villagers who stood watching helplessly below.

The woman was never seen again, but her memory lived for many years and in 1889 the rector of Leverington recorded that Mid-Lent Sunday was still known in his village as 'Whirling Sunday.' Some of his elderly parishioners could still dimly remember when a pleasure fair was held at Leverington to commemorate that day, which was a general holiday with sports, games and boxing matches. One or two villagers were still making small cakes known as 'Whirling Cakes' in memory of the legend of the old woman being whirled over St Leonard's steeple.

LINCOLN

The Devil, the Imp and the East Wind

LINCOLN cathedral is said to be one of the finest medieval buildings in Europe. Upon completion the monks believed the devil could not resist being malicious to such a wonderful place of worship and that he viewed it with a sour and evil expression, hence the adage 'He looks as the devil over Lincoln.'

Its exposed situation and the rather dissolute life of some of the clergy centuries ago gave rise to the following legend.

The devil became friendly with the wind and they went together to the cathedral. Satan told his companion to wait outside whilst he went in to have a chat with the dean and chapter. The wind agreed and has been waiting ever since and one presumes the devil has found a lot to discuss with the dean and chapter! His intimate alliance with the wind suggests that he has taken the place of Odin, a heathen 'Prince of the Powers of the Air,' greatly honoured by the Vikings who settled in Eastern England.

The famous Lincolnshire Imp is one of many devils to be found in the cathedral and sits at the cleft of a pillar adjacent to the east window, above the Angel Choir. The following is a popular tale concerning its presence.

Once a strong wind brought two imps to see the newly built cathedral at Lincoln. The first, who was curious to see what such a holy place had to offer, slipped in unnoticed and was so amazed at what it saw and heard, that its heart turned to stone and the creature became rooted to the ground. The other imp went looking for its brother and unwittingly alighted on the shoulders of a witch, who flew around the ceiling and deposited the imp, which she turned to stone, on its now well known perch. The wind, which always seems to be blowing, still haunts the minster precincts waiting for the return of the imps.

Little St Hugh

CHAUCER developed 'Little St Hugh' as one of his Canterbury Tales and the original story was probably a popular piece of anti-sematic propaganda which circulated at the time when Edward I expelled the Jews from England in 1290.

Half way down the south aisle of Lincoln cathedral is the remains of the shrine of 'Little St Hugh,' said to have been murdered in 1255. At that time and in common with many other cities, Lincoln had a large and prosperous Jewish community which was blamed for the boy's death and subsequent communal revenge.

The eight years old boy was alleged to have been murdered by a Jew named Copin, who lived at the foot of Steep Hill, Lincoln, whose daughter enticed the little boy over the wall and into their garden with the promise of an apple. He was seized and brought before a mock jury, then later tortured, crucified and murdered. When the boy failed to return home his mother sent out a search party which discovered his body at the bottom of a well belonging to a Jew's house.

The King's Justiciary, John de Lexington, was in Lincoln at the time of the crime and ordered Copin to be seized and questioned. On a pardon for his life he is said to have confessed to the murder and explained that the child had been put to death in front of a great many Jews who had gathered at Lincoln for the occasion, to avenge the crucifixion of Christ. One of their number elected to represent Pilate had ordered the punishment and eventual execution of the boy. The prisoner also admitted that it was the custom of the Jews to sacrifice a Christian child in this fashion every year, which was a popular story of that time.

Copin's life was not pardoned and he was later tied to a horse's tail and dragged to Canwick Hill, where he was hanged with 18 rich Jews, whilst many more were imprisoned at Lincoln.

LINDSEY

Yallery Brown

THE folklorist who collected this tale from the wetlands at the end of the last century said it was told by an old man called Tom who blamed his disappointing life on a small creature whom he released from under a stone when he was 16 years old. The thing was neither boggart nor bogle, but gave him no peace in this lifetime and probably none in the next.

On summer evenings Tom used to enjoy walking along the path which went out into the broad silent fields and beside the supposedly haunted spinney with its myriad fairy stones and rings. One dark night in July he heard a terrible sobbing and thought someone had left their baby in the long grass. He searched over a wide area in vain and the crying grew louder. Then he heard a voice whimpering, 'Oh the stone, the great big stone on top!'

He eventually found a great flat slab hidden under a tangle of weeds, almost covered with earth. It was the type which the marsh people called 'Strangers' Tables' where the 'Strangers,' or 'Tiddy' people danced on moonlight nights. The voice called up again, but Tom feared the 'Strangers' and was scared to move the stone.

However, the sound was so plaintive that he gave in and there was a little creature lying on its back, no bigger than a one year old baby, its ancient face peering out of long tangled yellow hair, its skin the colour of freshly dug earth and its beard twisted all round its body. The creature was yellow and brown all over and said its name was 'Yallery Brown.'

The lad asked if it were a bogle and was told he should not ask, but whatever it was it would always be his friend. Yallery Brown offered to grant Tom a wish, and being work-shy the boy asked for a helping hand and thanked him. The creature replied angrily that it was never to be thanked and stamped its feet with rage. When it calmed down it told its saviour that if he ever needed help or got into trouble he had only to call, 'Yallery Brown, come from the ground I want you!' and he would come immediately. Then he vanished.

When Tom went to work the next morning all his work was already done and he sat happily with his hands in his pockets doing nothing. Yallery Brown had done it for him and did so every day, but people saw the little creature flitting about at night and noticed brushes and tools working by themselves. Just as Tom's work was done for him, theirs was undone and they complained to their master.

The boy tried to work but the brooms would not stay in his hands and the ploughs ran away from him. Yallery Brown would not go away and in the end Tom was sacked. He was so angry that he shook his fist and shouted, 'Yallery Brown, come from the earth, I want you!'

The little creature appeared and was told his help was no longer welcome and the boy thanked him to leave him alone. The tiny thing gave a nasty laugh and said that as he had been thanked he would never give his help again, but he had never promised to leave Tom alone and he never would. He should have left him under the stone where he could have done no harm.

Tom tried his hand at many jobs but things always went wrong, thanks to Yallery Brown. When he married his children died, his wife had a harsh tongue and his cattle never fattened. He could never get away from the 'Tiddy' thing and he never would. The creature's song was always ringing in his ears:

'Wo'k as thou wull
Thou'll niver do well;
Wo'k as thou mowt
Thou'll niver gain owt;
For harm an' mischance an' Yallery Brown
Thou's let oot thy-self fro' unner th' sto'an.'

LONG SUTTON

Dick Turpin the Highwayman

TURPIN'S crimes committed whilst living at Long Sutton played a vital role in his eventual execution at York in 1738.

He was born in 1706 at Hempstead, near Saffron Walden where he worked as a butcher and was always under suspicion with his dubious meat dealings. When the law was about to book him, he moved to Cambridge where he stayed for a time at the 'Three Tuns' in Castle Street. The excise men were soon looking for him, but he managed to slip away and settle at Long Sutton in 1737, first at the 'Bull Hotel' in the Market Place and later in a rented cottage close to the Post Office in the High Street. He passed himself off as a horse dealer called Palmer, being his mother's maiden name, and his stock was mostly that which he had stolen for himself.

Eventually Mr Delamere, the local magistrate, issued a warrant for his arrest on the charge of sheep stealing, but

Turpin alias Palmer knocked the arresting officer to the ground and escaped to Yorkshire, where 'Black Bess', his famous horse, died en route.

In October 1738 he was staying at the 'Cock Inn' in Welton and was caught shooting a game cock belonging to his landlord. Still known as Palmer, he was arrested and taken before the magistrate who ordered him to find sureties for his good behaviour, but being unable to comply, was sent to the House of Correction at Beverley and for the first time in his life Turpin was behind bars.

Mr Cowle the magistrate became suspicious of his prisoner and delved further into his past life. Palmer insisted that he was a butcher by trade and he and his family had lived at Long Sutton, but bad debts had forced him to move north.

A letter of enquiry was sent by special messenger addressed to Mr Delamere, the Long Sutton magistrate, who replied that John Palmer was accused of sheep stealing, but had escaped and since that time information had been received concerning his horse stealing activities. Delamere further stated that Palmer's whereabouts before his stay at Long Sutton were unknown, and none of his family had resided in this South Lincolnshire town.

The prisoner was moved to York Castle, when every effort was made to discover his past history and there was soon sufficient evidence to commit him to trial. Many witnesses came forward for the prosecution and then Turpin made the big mistake of writing a letter to his father. Turpin senior was in Chelmsford Prison and his letter was returned to the Essex post office with the postage unpaid. The woman who had taught Dick to read and write happened to see it, recognised his writing and revealed his true identity.

Sufficient evidence was found to hang Dick Turpin, who was executed at York on April 2nd 1738 aged 32 and buried in St George's Churchyard.

LOUTH

How 'Six-Pint Smith' Changed His Name

THE legendary John Smith is said to have lived at Louth in the mid 19th century. Each day he went to his favourite pub at noon, and drank the twelve half-pints of beer set on his table before the church clock had finished chiming. This earned him the nick-name 'Six-Pint Smith' until he increased it by another four!

At the time of the annual fair he wanted to buy some goods from a pedlar, but having insufficient money, suggested they should have a beer drinking contest, with the winner taking all the stock.

Being another robust drinker, the pedlar agreed to the wager and 'Six-Pint' drank his first pint before the merchant had lifted his glass. Not to be out-done the pedlar took a pint in each hand and drained first one and then the other without wiping his mouth. All the time he matched his two for Smith's one and eventually after gulping eight pints in a very short time, the man from Louth admitted defeat.

However, the pedlar replied that if Smith would care to climb Louth steeple, he would receive not only all his stock, but also the money which he jingled in his purse.

'Six-Pint' drank another two for Dutch courage and with ten pints of beer under his belt made his perilous ascent of the church steeple. Back on firm ground he looked round for the pedlar and his winnings, but the scoundrel had run off, taking Smith's overcoat with him. The angry man cursed him and then remembered he had left his hat on top of the steeple and set off to retrieve it, but some soldiers took pot shots at it and the ruined article was left to decorate the church.

This daring wager elevated Smith's name to 'Ten-Pint Smith' and he lived up to his reputation!

MANEA

The 'Viking Ship'

THE Vikings found the east coast of England an easy target for their forays across the North Sea.

Manea is a very isolated village which lies close to the Hundred Foot washes, and it was here that Charles I intended to build his new 'Kingdom of Charlemont,' after the drainage of the Fens, but was beheaded before his plans were finished.

An old man who died in 1875 told his friend of an occasion in his youth when he was picking flowers out of D'Arcy Lode and two things rose up and scared him almost to death. He thought they were serpents, but upon closer investigation they looked like the stem and stern of a big boat or even a small ship.

His grandfather had laughed when he described how the things had risen up and the old man explained that they were in their proper place and the Fens were sinking.

The pieces of wood were taken home, broken up, dried out and used for kindling throughout the next winter. With hindsight the narrator thought the boat looked like those used by the 'foreigners who used to sail about these parts.' Who knows, perhaps the Harris family had burned the remains of a Viking longboat?

MARCH

The Devil and the 'Men Of March'

THE base of an old stone cross, which was probably a preaching cross, stands at the junction of the High Street and the Causeway, where according to legend it is said to mark the spot where a church was to be built. Each time a little progress was made, unaccountable disaster struck and soon it was rumoured to be the devil's work as he resented a house of God being placed in March.

Despite the gossip, building continued on and off for several years but with so many mishaps that it was eventually agreed to stop work. However, being true Fenmen, the 'Men of March', as some still like to be called, refused to be beaten. A stone crucifix was placed close to the site, the remains of which stand to this day as an object of terror to the devil who was never seen again.

In time a place of worship was successfully completed. This could have been the site of the beautiful 14th century church dedicated to St Wendreda, located about a mile north of the cross, which until 1855 came within the parish of Doddington. The building is believed to stand on the site of at least two previous churches, which formed the centre of the Early Saxon settlement of Merche, or March.

St Wendreda's has a double-hammerbeam angel roof reputed to be the finest example of its type in England. The heavenly creatures are so wonderful that I sometimes wait for them to ruffle their wings and whisper 'Well done!' to the 'Men of March' who cocked a snook at the devil.

MARSHLAND ST JAMES

The Giant Hickathrift

THE legendary giant Tom Hickathrift is said to have been born at Marshland St. James during the late Saxon period. He was a lazy boy who sat by the fire eating his poor widowed mother out of house and home. When he was ten years old he was six feet high, three feet wide, his hands were like a shoulder of mutton and he ate as much as five ordinary men.

A farmer offered the woman fresh straw for her mattresses and reluctantly Tom, who was invited to carry as much as he could manage, set off with a cart rope and came home with most of the field on his back. Soon his strength became well known and after a little bribery a brewer from Lynn successfully hired him and Tom was making the 20 mile journey each day carting beer to Wisbech and the marshes.

There was a shorter route which he decided to use which cut across the marsh, now known as the Smeeth, which was guarded by a monstrous giant who either killed all trespassers or made them his slaves.

Tom flung open the gates of the giant's vast estate and was challenged to a fight. Whilst his adversary went off to his cave to fetch his club, Tom turned his cart upside down, taking the axle-tree and wheel for his sword and buckler. After a gruelling fight, he cut off the giant's head and returned home with all his treasure.

The youth was a hero, for the giant had been a great enemy to that part of the country and celebratory bonfires were lit for miles around. He was no longer called plain

Tom, but Mr Hickathrift and received the giant's estate and wealth.

The cave was demolished and a large house built on the site surrounded by a vast estate to maintain Tom and his mother. He gave the remainder of the land to the poor for their common and built a church close by which was dedicated to St James, for it was on that saint's Feast Day that he rid the Smeeth of its ogre.

Sometime afterwards, as he was walking about his estate, he met upon the outskirts of the forest a well-built tinker called Henry Nonsuch, who had a great dog to carry his bag of tools. Tom challenged the trespasser and lost the fight, but they became boon companions and together performed many heroic feats, including quelling an uprising of some 10,000 people at Ely, which earned Tom a knighthood and Henry a king's pension of 40 shillings a year.

Hickathrift is said to have determined his burial place by throwing a stone from his home, which landed to the east of Tilney All Saints churchyard. This is where his unmarked 8 ft long stone slabbed grave lies at right angles with the pathway and is often tangled with grass in the summer. To the south is his 'candlestick' (the upright of an old memorial or preaching cross) and he is depicted on the village sign which stands beside the church.

Tom and Henry are also carved on the Marshland St James sign at Hickathrift Crossroads, at the junction of Walton Road and School Road with Smeeth Road. Until the early 1980s a large indentation known as 'Hickathrift's Washbasin' lay partially in the first field to the left of School Road, before it was filled in for housing development and partially in the garden of the adjoining 'Hickathrift House.' A large stone named 'Hickathrift's Collar Stud' so called because of its shape stood close by, but vanished in the late 1950s or early 1960s.

More of his artefacts can be seen in two villages off the A47 King's Lynn Road. Another 'candlestick' stands in the garden of Terrington St John's vicarage, next to the north door of the church, and the small effigy, possibly of Roman origin, carved on the outside corner of the north chancel wall at Walpole St Peter's, is traditionally believed to represent the giant. The indentation in the wall to its left is supposed to have been made when Tom threw either a cannonball or a round stone at the devil, who was lurking in the churchyard. He is also held responsible for trying to steal the church tower at West Walton, hence it being separate from the main building although another legend blames the devil who apparently could not stand the sound of its bells!

THE METHWOLD SEVERALS

The Legend of Mucky Porter

THE Methwold Severals is a large area of agricultural land flanked by the B1160 Southery to Wereham Road, the river Wissey and Methwold Common.

According to this traditional tale, Mucky Porter was the first owner of this fertile area and this is how he acquired it:–

During the reign of Charles I Porter kept the 'Fleece' tavern at Southery and was also hired to take travellers across the perilous, undrained fens. On the 1st May, 1646, Sir Ralph Skipworth of Snowre Hall, Fordham, sent his servant to fetch Master Porter, who swore his loyalty to the Crown. Charles I was hiding from Cromwell's troops at the Hall and it was agreed that Mucky would escort him to Huntingdon, where he would take leave and the monarch travel on to Oxford.

His majesty was disguised in peasant clothing and they rode all day and well into the night until they reached their first destination at the Manor of Wentworth, some 4½ miles west of Ely, where they were given shelter.

They set off early the next morning and were just approaching Histon when the guide saw some Round-heads in the distance heading their way. He and the king managed to get their mounts through a thick hedge and took shelter in an osier bed on the other side. This place became known as 'King's Hedges' which is now a large urban area within the northern city boundary of Cambridge. They did not reach Huntingdon until midnight, where Mucky Porter was given a bag of gold for his trouble.

Time passed and then one day a stranger called at the 'Fleece' with news that King Charles had been beheaded. The unwelcome Dutchmen came and drained the Fens and the innkeeper's adventures were but a memory. After the Restoration in 1660, two strangers called to inform him that the new king, Charles II, had decreed that Mucky Porter, who had bravely assisted his father, was to select a portion of the newly drained Methwold Fen as farmland for himself and his successors.

Porter chose his land by rule of thumb, then enquired as to how many acres were his. 'Without measuring I cannot say,' replied one of the king's agents, 'But there are several' and this land has been called the 'Methwold Severals' ever since!

MUMBY

The Farmer and the Boggart

THERE was once a farmer from Mumby, near Alford, who bought a large field adjoining his land. Soon after the purchase a squat, long-armed hairy little boggart ordered him to quit his land. The man refused, saying it was his and they argued for sometime until the farmer said he would take it to law. The boggart refused and suggested they share the crops.

The farmer agreed and asked him what he would like, that which grew above or below the ground, but in either case he could not change his mind once his decision had been made.

The boggart thought carefully and settled for the top, so the cunning farmer set potatoes and waited for the crop to grow. When the little creature came to collect his share at harvest, there was a huge pile of potatoes belonging to the farmer in one corner of the field and a pile of old stalks for himself in another.

The creature was very angry but eventually calmed down and the farmer enquired what part he would like for the next harvest. He said he would have the bottoms and the man could have the tops. So the farmer sowed wheat and claimed the grain and the other had the stubble.

The boggart insisted that wheat was sown again for the next season and they should mow together, taking whatever each of them harvested. As late summer approached the greedy farmer, who had no intention of sharing his crop, consulted the village wise-woman who told him to lay iron rods in the boggart's side of the field which would blunt his scythe.

The farmer streaked ahead with his mowing whilst his partner had to keep stopping to use the whet-stone and

64

in the end the boggart shouted out that he could keep the lot and vanished down a big hole. He never came back to claim the land, but for years after he scared people in the dark and stole anything which was left lying on the ground.

MURROW

The Cromwell Connection

ALMOST half way down Silvers Lane at OS TF143 383080 is a small tree clad mound adjacent to the lane and known as the 'Ghost Hill.' This is where, within memory, Oliver Cromwell's ghost was seen wandering on dark nights and was a very frightening place for walkers and cyclists.

It is said that 'Old Noll' as Cromwell was called in the Fens, had a cannon placed on this mound during the Civil War trained on the church of St John the Baptist at Church End Parson Drove, some 4/5ths of a mile away. Although the church remained unharmed, his ghost wandered about in retribution for his intended crime. It is said you could conjure up his spirit by walking around the mound 10 times, but no one seems to have tried it.

The same ghost is also said to haunt Rabbit Hill at OS TF143 448108 on the Dowgate Road, Leverington, which is another putative cannon site, this time with St Leonard's church as its target.

Some of the elderly villagers of Sutton St James close by believe that Cromwell was responsible for their church steeple being detached from the main building. Apparently he placed his gun next to the Butter Cross, took a pot shot at the steeple about a mile distant and badly damaged it. A replacement was built but nobody bothered to put it back in its rightful position!

THE NENE WASHES

The Plover Hole Mystery

THE Nene Washes take the floodwater from the river Nene and the 12 miles long drainage channel, Morton's Leam, cut by Bishop Morton, Abbot of Ely in 1480, which starts at Stanground, Peterborough and finishes at Guyhirn.

The 'Plover Hole,' is located at OS TF142 365017 and although there is no public access, it can be seen from the river bank approached from the un-named lane leading to the left of the A47 Wisbech to Peterborough Road at its junction with the Parson Drove road, some 2½ miles from Guyhirn Bridge. Permission to walk this bank must be obtained from the farmer at Elm Tree Farm, at the end of the lane.

As dusk fell on 23rd November 1956, a party of two local farmers, a gunsmith and a veterinary surgeon, had a very strange experience when they were out shooting wigeon in the Plover Hole which lies in a shallow depression and they still cannot work it out.

As usual they had punted across the Nene and the still weather conditions and hint of moonlight were ideal for a good night's sport. They were also keeping watch for Jack Wymer, aged 42, a notorious Wisbech poacher who was quite likely to be out on the Washes. Jack, now separated from his family, lived with Bet his devoted black labrador bitch, in a tiny flat in the former Midlands Counties hotel which stood on the site of the petrol filling-station in Chapel Road.

They placed themselves about 40 yards apart and it was not long before the intruder was seen roughly 120 yards away, walking over the river bank. It was strange that Bet was not with him for usually they were inseparable. He walked boldly towards them and when he was some 10 yards away one of the wildfowlers shone his torch on him, whereupon he vanished.

When the light was extinguished he could again be seen quite clearly walking along the bank. Again the torch was shone on him and he disappeared. This was repeated three times and by now all the sportsmen were stalking the figure.

About 70 yards away there was a very steep drain which had no bridge, so it was impossible to cross at that point without walking back up the bank and going over a stile. It was some 4 feet deep and perhaps 20 feet across with a barbed wire fence on both sides. The figure was walking in a straight line towards it, as if it were not there. His pursuers were almost at his heels when he vanished. He did not scramble down its high bank and he certainly did not cross the water. Nor did he retrace his steps or walk over the river bank.

The onlookers were totally puzzled, especially when they checked distances and discovered it was impossible to see a man from 120 yards as they had when the poacher was first discovered. However, they were convinced this was no trick of the imagination as all four had seen what they were beginning to think was an apparition. Later they wondered if it had been a spectral premonition, for exactly one week later, to the night, Jack Wymer whom they were convinced they had seen at the Plover Hole, although not necessarily in the flesh, committed suicide at home.

NORTH LINCOLNSHIRE

The Dead Hand

BEFORE the Lincolnshire wet-lands were drained in the 17th century people were scared to cross them at night unless they carried spells, or a safe-keep, to protect them from the evils which lived in the waterholes. These were often a Bible verse written on paper which was crinkled up in a nutshell or words composed by a wise-woman.

The fate of Long Tom Pattison strengthened the need for protection. This foolish lad used to tease his companions for being so superstitious and eventually they told him to prove there was no evil or keep quiet forever. Eventually it was settled that Tom would demonstrate his bravery the next night by walking the path across the bogs and round by every willow-snag.

He was so confident that some of the young boys thought the horrors might not be as black as they were painted, but the old people knew better and shook their heads and hoped no harm would come from his foolish, disbelieving ways.

A large crowd gathered outside his mother's cottage to see if he really would accept the challenge and saw her trying to put something into his pocket. But Tom refused her spells, snatched the lantern from her and ran off laughing towards the bog-lands.

Some of the men tried to stop him but Long Tom only laughed in their faces, so they went home and hoped for the best. However, some of the young ones decided to follow him down the path which led to the marshes. Tom was about 30 yards ahead and as they came to the willow snag the wind started to moan and a damp chill came from the sea. His lantern went out and he stood motionless in the dark whilst his followers trembled and prayed, holding onto their safe-keeps, waiting for whatever would happen.

Then Tom was surrounded by evil things and the once still night was full of moving shadows and dim grinning faces with blazing eyes and wailing voices. The boys could not see Tom but heard him swearing and shouting. Then he appeared to be fighting with the horrors. Suddenly a light appeared and they could see Long Tom's deathly white face, as he held on to a willow with one hand, his other stretched out and clasped in a hand without a body, known as the Dead Hand, which pulled him towards the black bog beyond the path. Then with a terrible shriek he vanished into the water.

The boys eventually found their way home and the next morning a search party went in vain to look for the missing youth. Day after day they walked the marshes and Tom's mother became so demented that people became scared of her and left her alone for she moved around like one of the bog things herself.

A month passed and one evening, just before twilight, the old woman was seen running along the marsh path, shouting and beckoning to be followed and although very scared, some people went after her. She led them to her son who was sitting with his feet in the water and his back against the snag, looking like a wizened old man. He kept pointing and gibbering at the horrors which only he could see and where the other hand ought to have been, the one which had been gripped by the Dead Hand, there was nothing but a ragged stump.

Nobody ever knew where he had been or why he had come back, for Long Tom Pattison never spoke a word again, but sat alone by day and went running into the marshes at night and was dead within a year.

He was found lying in his mother's lap and she too was dead, with a contented expression on her face. But they said Tom looked as if the horrors had taken him and they said he haunted the marshes on dark nights before the marshes were drained. The woman always trailed behind him, calling out her pleasure that her son had come back to his poor old widowed mother.

OUTWELL

Beaupre Hall

THE 16th century Beaupre Hall which stood to the north of the village and east of the A1101 Wisbech to Downham Market road at OS TF143 515046, was demolished in the 1960s. One of its most remarkable owners was the eccentric Beaupre Bell, who became High Sheriff of Norfolk in 1706. He almost starved his son to death and kept over 500 wild horses in the Park, all having the free run of his mansion.

Two stone eagles sat on top of the gateposts, which were a fine feature of the large sweeping front drive, but these were no ordinary monumental birds, for within memory they were said to flap their wings at midnight and swoop from their perches to drink from the nearby water course. On certain nights some villagers also saw an unidentified passenger leave the hall in the 'Opal Coach' at midnight, pulled at terrific speed by two headless horses, whipped on by a black clothed driver, always heading towards St Clement's church. Another version of this tale says that anyone passing the Hall gates just after midnight would see a row of carriages drawn up, all with headless coachmen.

One of the bedrooms was greatly feared for every day the bed was made and although the room was unoccupied, some unknown person slept in it each night. The servants never dared leave it unmade in case the mysterious sleeper should haunt the house.

A different bedroom tale foretold bad luck to the master of Beaupre Hall and his servants if any bed was left unmade after 11.00 am. This goes back to the time when one of the owners supposedly found his bedroom in a dishevilled state at that hour of day. He grabbed hold of the lazy, or perhaps over-worked, offending girl and pushed her down the stairs, where she was left to die on the hall floor. Her bloodstains remained for many years despite frequent scrubbing and it is she who cursed the place when beds lay crumpled after hours, in retribution for her own murder.

PARSON DROVE

The Woman With a 'Holy Hand'

SUE WISEMAN alias 'Happy Sue,' or 'Holy Hannah,' was born at Parson Drove sometime in the 1870s. Her home was a little wooden bungalow, the first on the right at Highside going from Parson Drove towards Leverington Common, which has now been extended and rendered. Her right hand was always swathed in red flannel. She called it her 'holy hand' which she claimed had touched Jesus and had been bandaged ever since to keep the holiness in. She used this one to hold the tambourine which never left her side and was banged for most of her waking hours.

Many Fenland people feared this strange little 'witchy-woman' as some still call her, who was always dressed in a stained skirt which almost touched the ground, an old coat with a piece of string tied around her waist and an ancient, floppy brimmed hat pulled over her whispy, dirty grey hair. If anyone displeased her she would curse them, and she scared children half to death.

It is rumoured that one winter night, when Sue was young, she met an itinerant who was dossing down in a farmer's stackyard. Their brief union resulted in a child, whom she named Jesus, but she was considered to be an unfit mother so the child was taken away and she kept her sorrow to herself.

Sue walked for miles, either talking to herself or any passersby about hell and damnation, shaking her tambourine, leaping out on men as they left the pubs at night and sleeping rough for weeks on end. Sometimes she was accompanied by one of her two friends, but never the two together. There was Liz Carmen, who never missed walking from her village, Sutton St Edmund, to Parson Drove each Sunday for worship at the Salvation Army hut and was particularly fond of her bonnet. Liz liked to dance to the tambourine and would jump up and down like a little performing dog. The other, who was almost as eccentric as Sue, was Mrs Benstead from Dowsdale Bank near Crowland.

People dreaded hearing Sue shuffling up their paths at dinner time for they knew she had come to cadge a meal and were scared to refuse because of her curses. Neither did she ever go cold for she would bang on doors and say, 'The Lord has sent me for a few sticks,' and the unlucky householder would have to go out no matter the time or weather to meet her request or bear her wrath. Even a bus journey to Wisbech from Parson Drove on Mr Morton Hunter's luxurious bus known as 'Lady Comfey' was a greater experience when the percussive woman was on board, for she rarely dipped into her purse. Instead she caused a tremendous commotion and usually managed to get a free ride.

For countless years Sue Wiseman jingled and rattled in her own red flannelled fashion, through towns and villages, down droves and across dykes. She was buried at Southsea church on 6th November, 1936 in an unmarked pauper's grave towards the hedge boundary with the new Methodist chapel. Sue lies between Thomas William Jacobs and Desmond Stanley Hall and, now an established part of Fenland folklore, is still remembered with cautious affection.

PETERBOROUGH

The Museum Ghost

THE Peterborough Museum and Art Gallery in Priestgate was once the town house of the Earls Fitzwilliam and later became the town infirmary. On many occasions nurses complained they heard strange inexplicable footsteps coming from the upper corridors.

It was reported in the Peterborough Citizen on 3rd May, 1932 that the Museum caretaker's wife, Mrs Yarrow and their daughter were often aware of someone walking across the Norman Cross Room at night, which was once the Women's Surgical Ward. Mrs Yarrow said the footsteps began at 8 pm and ceased with the closing of a door at about 9.30 pm. The noise was more intense at the waning of the moon.

They nick-named the ghost 'Thomas' as he first appeared on St Thomas Day, 21st December. He was not troublesome and was seen in the corridor which separated the caretaker's bedrooms from the Norman Cross Room. Mrs Yarrow had just gone through the double doors which led to the kitchen, and happened to look 'half-left' and saw the ghost standing there. She could not distinguish his features, which had a phosphorescent glow, but he was dressed in a modern light grey suit. Then he vanished into thin air. The corridor was dimly lit through a fan light, but Mrs Yarrow was adamant that she saw him then, as on many subsequent occasions, as plainly as any mortal.

In another article printed that year her daughter told the reporter how she had got out of bed in what had been the old House Surgeon's Room to investigate a strange noise she heard in the corridor.

She saw a young, tall good looking man dressed in a light grey suit standing in the corridor and called out to him, quite unafraid. He neither answered nor turned round, but floated through the doors at the end of the passage which led to the Norman Cross Room. She called for her father and they checked the doors, which were still locked.

People came from miles around to stand outside the Museum under the waning moon to catch sight of 'Thomas,' but he never obliged. When the Yarrows left he was never seen again, but a member of staff told the *Peterborough Citizen & Advertiser* in October, 1973 that he often heard footsteps when he was alone and could find no evidence of other people being in the vicinity. One of his colleagues also swore that he could hear someone walking in one of the upstairs rooms.

It is said that in time the original owner hated being anywhere near his wife, so had another house built nearby for her and lived by himself. Perhaps he is angry because the solitude of his house has been broken?

QUEEN ADELAIDE

The Bee Woman

QUEEN ADELAIDE lies to the north east of Ely and the large factory adjacent to the bank of the river Great Ouse is built on land once known as Turburtsea Island before the Fens were drained.

This was a tiny island and not far from Ely where some legendary knights came seeking largesse to fight their foreign wars. They soon became bored with the celibate hospitality at the abbey and when a monk told them about the beautiful wife of the shepherd from Turburtsea Island who spent a lot of time from home, the bravest knight agreed to kidnap her and bring her back to the abbey.

The young woman never feared her husband's long absences and spent many hours talking to her bees and making mead from their honey which she sold to the abbey. She was working on her hives when the knight thundered down her track and from her hiding place watched him dismount, pull his visor down to conceal his identity and walk into her hut.

He helped himself to the mead which lay in a large bowl on the kitchen table and drank so greedily that some splashed on his breast-plate. Even more brave with strong liquor, he went in search of his prey and dragged her screaming and kicking from behind the bee hives. Her cries for mercy fell on deaf ears. But just as she was about to be tied to his black horse she called to her bees in a strange low voice.

They responded at once and great swarms flew towards the knight, attracted to the honey spilled on his armour. They crawled through every chink, stinging him as he ran into the river where he was drowned by the weight of his chain mail. The woman's honour remained intact and she continued to live in harmony with her bees who guarded her with extra care.

RAMSEY

The Founding of Ramsey Abbey

IF this legend is true, Ramsey Abbey is the result of the dream of a fisherman who earned his living at Ramsey Mere. One day he was unable to catch any fish, so being totally exhausted he lay down in his boat and went to sleep. He dreamed that St Benedict told him to cast his net the following dawn and it would soon be full. The largest fish would be a 'Hacaed', which he was to take to his master Ailwin as a gift from St Benedict and tell him that from his vast wealth he was to build a religious house. The site of this building was to be determined as follows:

Ailwin was to closely observe how the animals on the island lay down when they were tired, and the altar of the church was to be placed on the spot where a bull would tear up a piece of land. As a measure of truth the saint would cure Ailwin of his chronic gout. Then he bent the little finger of the fisherman which he said Ailwin would be able to straighten.

The following dawn the fisherman did as he was told and his haul was so large he could hardly land the net. The largest fish was selected and presented to Ailwin, who was informed of the strange dream. He listened with great interest and was able to straighten the fisherman's finger. Fully convinced that he had received a holy commission, he thanked God and St Benedict for the honour.

He took his boat and journeyed to the island, rejoicing that he was now free from chronic pain. When he reached dry land he saw that all his cattle were lying in the shape of a cross and a bull was in the middle. When the animal saw the man it stood up and struck the ground three hard blows with its foot.

Ailwin was now convinced that the fisherman's story was true and at once set about building a monastery. Today its ruins still stand on the edge of the town.

RAVELEY

Mr Leech and the Devil

THE Raveleys are a group of villages which stand above the Fens and lie to the south of Ramsey off the B1040 St Ives to Crowland road. In 1662 a tract was printed concerning what was claimed to be a true account of the misfortune which befell Farmer John Leech from Raveley.

It happened at the time of the Whittlesey Fair, which the farmer intended visiting after his customary morning visit to the inn, where he met an old friend who became annoyed by his drunken behaviour and made to leave. Leech called for more drinks and shouted, 'Let the devil take him who goeth out of this house today,' and so his patient friend stayed on. The farmer eventually decided to set off across the fens to the fair, but his companion reminded him of his oath. The drunkard laughed and said the devil would not trouble him and besides he was far too heavy to be carried half way to the fair. 'But he will be able to carry you to your journey's end somewhere else,' replied his friend.

Leech dismissed him and with difficulty rode off towards Whittlesey. He had travelled no more than two miles when he suddenly remembered his boast back at the inn, which he regretted. He became so frightened that he did not know what to do and rode around in circles until night fell.

Just before midnight and still mounted on his poor half-dead horse, two griffins came out from the shadows and barred his way. Then presently he heard a terrible voice, which reminded him three times of his sins and the oath he had broken that day. Leech fell down in a trance and two little devils jumped out from behind a hedge and beat him. Then they tore at his clothes, gripped him by the arms and flew up in the sky with the struggling farmer and carried him many miles over Whittlesey Mere to Doddington near March and dropped him senseless in the Patron's Yard.

The next morning some farmworkers found the dazed and naked man soaked with blood, impaled on some plough harrows. He was taken to their master's house and given medical attention and in time was able to narrate his strange story and begged that he might stay for a further two days before returning to Raveley. His request was granted and that same morning some of his torn clothing was found two miles away.

Leech went berserk when he saw the garments and his host had to send for the parson, who he viciously attacked. He had to be tied to his bed and locked in. The next morning all was quiet and so the door was opened. Farmer Leech was still tied to the bed, but his neck was broken. His blackened body was swollen to double its size with every bone out of joint.

This ghastly spectacle drew hordes of people to congregate around his deathbed and speculate over the devil's handiwork. For many years John Leech's ordeal was held as an example to all men who make wild oaths when deep in their cups.

SKEGNESS

A Ghostly Experience at Skegness Railway Station

ONE Sunday afternoon in early September 1978, Mark was sitting in an empty train parked alongside platform 6 of the Skegness British Rail Station doing his homework. One of his hobbies was railways and as most of his family worked in this industry he got to know the staff at this station. He was often allowed to visit the signal boxes and even ride up front with the driver and loved trains so much that he was sometimes allowed to sit in an empty one on a Sunday afternoon and study.

For much of the time this was a quiet day, but during the summer season the station was busy early in the morning when the tourists arrived destined for the beach and again in the evening, when they returned home, dragging their weary children behind them. The empty excursion trains stayed parked in this small terminus station, which was an ideal opportunity for the boy to enjoy his pastime and keep his teachers and parents happy.

He was busy doing his school work seated in the Shrewsbury excursion train, which was not scheduled to depart for another three hours and as the next train was not due to arrive for another two hours the station was dead. All the platform gates were locked from the departure side, so imagine Mark's surprise when he got out of his seat and saw an old woman standing half-way down the centre aisle of the coach. She was wearing a very old fashioned purple dress, had a very haggard face and seemed very unsure of where she was and what she was doing.

He shyly asked her where she was going but received no reply. Turning his head for a split second, she vanished.

It was impossible for her to have left the train in the conventional method, for either way there was the long aisle to negotiate before reaching the carriage doors. Even a young athlete could not have made it in the time it took to turn a head.

Mark walked down the platform on to the station front, but still the gates remained locked from his side and there was no sign of the mysterious woman on the station concourse. The question remains, who was she and what was she doing and did he really share a carriage on the parked excursion train with a ghost? He thinks he probably did.

SKELLINGTHORPE

The Tale of a Brave Dog

WHEN Henry Stone of Skellingthorpe died in 1693, he left instructions to be buried as near to the church wall as possible, so that his faithful dog, which outlived him, could eventually be buried close to him on unconsecrated ground. Henry Stone was deeply indebted to this animal and his tomb still stands in the churchyard.

They were caught in a violent thunderstorm when walking in the fields one afternoon in 1690. Mr Stone quickly took shelter under a large oak tree, but his pet immediately pulled him out into the torrential rain. The bemused man returned to his cover and as soon as the dog had pulled him away for the third time, the tree was blown to smithereens by a huge fork of lightning, which killed a pheasant sheltering in its branches.

He owed his life to his wonderful dog and had its portrait painted to commemorate the event. The picture can be seen above the mantelpiece in the Blue Drawing Room at Doddington Hall and shows the dog, the tree and the pheasant.

SOHAM

Joseph Hempsall's Ghost

JOSEPH HEMPSALL had a farm close to the edge of Soham Mere. Before it was drained in the 17th century it was some 1000 acres of water and wetland which teemed with wildlife and prosperity. It was also a place to be avoided on dark nights when it claimed many lives.

Joe walked most nights across the mere to a tavern at Wicken and was one of the few men able to pick their way across the swamps on moonless nights. He was a true 'Fen Slodger', jumping dykes with his long leaping pole and walking around the edge of the sinister Big-Bog with complete confidence.

One night when he was over at Wicken, a thick fog clamped down and his mates begged him not to cross the mere, but to stay the night at the inn or even take the long walk along the trackway. However, the obstinate man put on his coat and started his perilous journey in the thickest fog within memory, which lasted three days and nights. His lamp shone eerily as he left the warm room and he whistled for comfort as he headed towards Big-Bog.

On the fourth morning the fog cleared and the sun came out, so one of the Wicken men set out to visit Hempsall's farm to make sure he had returned safely. Just as he was approaching the farm he was met by Joe, looking strange and bent, who did not say a word until they reached the farmhouse door. Then he looked round with vacant staring eyes and said in a strange voice, 'Enter not, for my body lies in Big-Bog.

As the poor visitor turned to run, Joe put an icy hand on his and continued, 'As I be now, so one day shall ye be. Go to the big dyke and find there my body.'

The frightened man went to Big-Bog and sure enough, there was Joseph Hempsall's body with a terrible expression on its face, lying half in and half out of the big reed-choked dyke.

Half crazed with terror he raced back to Wicken, and at last he was able to tell his tale. His friends set off without him to retrieve the corpse and although they searched in what they believed to be the right place found nothing. They assumed their friend had been playing tricks and headed back for Wicken.

Joe suddenly appeared from nowhere and said in his new voice, 'As I be now, so one day shall ye all be. Recover my body from the west side of Big-Bog and bury it in Wicken Churchyard.' Then a huge black cloud came down and swallowed up the apparition. In a short time the party came to the big dyke and true enough, there was the body with its terrible expression lying half in and half out of the water.

Joseph Hempsall was taken back to Soham and buried in the churchyard there. But for many years his spirit haunted the lonely fen between Soham and Wicken, reminding people that 'As I be now, so one day shall ye all be.' According to legend Hempsall will continue to haunt until his body rests in Wicken soil.

SOUTH ELKINGTON

The Green Lady of Thorpe Hall

'THE Spanish Lady's Love' is one of three ballads printed together in Percy's *Reliques* and gives an idea of the national spirit of the war with Spain and the good conduct of the English forces in the 16th century.

The Spanish lady is believed to be Donna Leonora Oveido or the 'Green Lady' which still haunts the 16th century Thorpe Hall, near Louth. One of her favourite places is around the 'Five Sisters' sycamore tree which has five trunks growing from its base and stands in the deer park.

She was taken prisoner during the Siege of Cadiz in 1587 and placed in the custody of John Bolle, the first owner of Thorpe Hall, who was knighted for his bravery in Spain. He treated her with kindness and she is said to have fallen in love with him and begged him to marry her and take her back to England. Not wishing to offend or embarrass the senorita, Bolle made the reply that he was unable as he had no money. Donna Leonora gave him all her jewellery and £500, but he still declined, this time using the excuse that the sea crossing would exhaust a well bred woman. Donna Leonora refused to listen to his excuses and eventually John Bolle had to confess that he was already married.

The dispirited woman joined a nunnery and insisted that he accept all her treasure as a gift for his wife. He received the presents and as he took his leave, Donna Leonora handed him a tiny portrait of herself, painted on a wooden panel in a gilt frame. She was dressed in green, playing a guitar in the company of her ladies and told Bolle to keep it forever.

On his return to England, his wife graciously accepted the gifts and the portrait was hung on the drawing room wall. It was not long before its ghostly double was seen walking about the house and its grounds. The apparition was dubbed 'The Green Lady' and there was no question of removing the picture, which remained at Thorpe Hall for a further 154 years after Sir John's death in 1606.

The figure is seen on occasions about the hall and the adjacent road and the present owners have found evidence of a handgate in the wall at her favourite point of egress. They also say that although smoking is prohibited, sometimes around nine o'clock at night the smell of cigar smoke drifts from the dining room. Perhaps it is a reminder of long past dinners when the first master of Thorpe Hall and his companions enjoyed their tobacco, introduced by his commanding officer, Sir Francis Drake. Maybe he spoke of the Siege of Cadiz and the passionate Spanish lady whom he unwittingly brought to England in a frame of gilt.

SOUTHERY

Black Shuck

BLACK SHUCK, the legendary spectral hound, is said to haunt many parts of East Anglia and one of his favourite places is Southery. Sometimes known as the 'Hateful Thing' he came to our shores as Viking mythology, being the Hound of Odin, the God of War and the Lord of Valhalla.

When you are walking alone in the Fens on dark nights it is easy to believe in Shuck's existence under that great dark sky with only flat fields and sudden noises for company. The emptiness makes you vulnerable to ancient superstitions.

The beast is still seen on occasions roaming about in the dark, his cyclops eye glowing red and sometimes yellow. Others say he has two eyes which change from red to yellow in sequence. He has also been seen with his head hovering over his body and his howl usually presages death.

Andrew Cochrane thinks Black Shuck followed him one late afternoon in winter during the Second World War. He was riding his AJS motor bike from Littleport to Downham Market and noticed his fuel gauge was pointing to empty as he was passing through Southery. He knew he would not be able to fill up until he reached Downham Market and was all alone when the inevitable happened a few moments later and he ran out of petrol. So he set off to push the machine 6 miles to home.

Presently the rhythmic sound of boots and tyres were joined by the padding feet of a large animal trailing a heavy chain. Andrew did not dare look round, for he was certain it was Black Shuck. So he walked faster, as did his pursuer. Then he slacked his pace for a brief moment, the 'Hateful Thing' copied him and the next village was nearly three miles away. The man was running for his life, still pushing the AJS, when a fuel tanker came down the road destined for the American Air Base at Mildenhall. The driver was flagged down and told the frightful tale, but of course the ghost dog had disappeared. Fortunately for Cochrane, the driver was understanding and gave him a little aviation fuel, which although not ideal was all right for a short journey. He arrived home in one piece and to this day is convinced that Black Shuck stalked him over 50 years ago.

STAMFORD

The Legend of the Brazenose Knocker

AS the town prospered in the 12th and 13th centuries a new university was built and Stamford became the country's third most important medieval university after Oxford and Cambridge. Between 1333 and 1335 a group of dissident masters and students broke away from Oxford University and moved here following the dissolution of their alternative university at Northampton. In 1334 Oxford persuaded King Edward III to close Stamford down and despite great local resistance its remaining scholars and masters were finally expelled in July 1335.

The breakaway group had brought the knocker from Brazenose College, Oxford with them and attached it to the gate of the new Brazenose College which stood on St Paul's Street close to its junction with East Street, but the following legend has another explanation.

Friar Roger Bacon, the great scholar, scientist, alchemist and necromancer, also known as 'Doctor Mirabilis' for his vast skills and learning, is said to have been a fellow of the Stamford Brazenose College. During this time he decided that the town would be magnificently protected against enemy action if it had a wall of brass erected around its perimeter. He would gain his knowledge by first fashioning a miraculous head of brass which would tell him how to build the fortification.

He and his friend Friar Bungay who was to assist him consulted their demon mentor who gave them the secret for making the head, which would speak briefly after one month. They laboured hard and eventually the work was done and the magic artefact attached to the college gate.

By now Bacon and Bungay were exhausted and ordered their servant to watch over the bronze head whilst they slept and awaken them should it start speaking. Unfortunately he grew tired from his tedious vigil and when the head spoke, saying 'Time is' he ignored it. It spoke again saying 'Time was' and still the servant did not awake his masters. Finally the head shouted, 'Time's past' and fell to the ground where it burst into tiny pieces. The noise awoke Roger Bacon who soon realised that his dream of building the wall of brass was shattered along with the bronze head.

The original door knocker brought from Oxford in the 14th century remained attached to the Brazenose Gate until it was removed and returned to its namesake in 1890, the original gate having been demolished in 1868. A Fellow of the Oxford college presented the town with a replica gate and knocker which can be seen on the old site, which records the secession of students of Brazenose Hall, Oxford to Stamford between 1333–35.

SWINESHEAD

Crazy Kate

THE 'Manwar Rings at OS TF131 244410 are thought to be a Danish encampment, or possibly earlier and are 60 yards in diameter surrounded by a double fosse. Years ago an old recluse named 'Crazy Kate' alleged to be a witch, visited these rings at night to commune with the devil.

She lived alone with her three cats, being her familiars, and was blamed for all the considerable ills and misfortunes which struck her neighbours. They decided to keep a close watch on her movements and for three successive days and nights hid in her garden, but saw nothing. On the fourth night a brave man looked through her window and still she could not be seen, so it was agreed that she had made a spell of invisibility and escaped.

The gang broke in and discovered the three familiars basking in front of the fire and a besom broom standing next to the hearth, which were all the trappings of a witch's home. They were debating their next move when Crazy Kate crept into the room, cursing the intruders who raced for the safety of the inn. Some wanted to burn the old woman along with her house and cats, but others thought it more prudent to run her out of Swineshead. A vote was taken and a note delivered giving her fourteen days notice to quit the district. But the messenger was cursed and ridiculed by Kate who promised misfortune to those who had crossed her threshold.

Illness and destruction struck Swineshead and following the death of a baby, the local preacher publicly denounced Kate and accused her of witchcraft and said more deaths would follow and no children would be safe in their parents' arms.

The congregation was fired up by his words and went back to the lonely cottage and finding it empty assumed she had been forewarned by the devil. They hunted in vain and as darkness fell, set out for the fearsome 'Manwar Rings' rumoured to be the haunt of witches and things best kept secret.

Crazy Kate was standing on the top bank as the vigilantes swarmed towards her. On her point of capture, a black cloaked stranger rode up the mound on a powerful black foam-lathered horse, whose hooves thundered and echoed around the encampment. The mysterious figure bent over, scooped Kate up in his arms and they rode away forever. Her home was burned down that night along with the cats who screamed like devils in the flames of revenge.

TYDD ST GILES

Hannath Hall

THIS village which lies on the borders of Cambridgeshire and Lincolnshire is famous for three things. The glorious Walsingham window in the parish church and the near certainty that in the 12th century Nicholas Breakspear, who was the only Englishman to be made Pope, was not only the curate of neighbouring Tydd St Mary, but also at one time curate of Tydd St Giles. He took the name Pope Adrian IV.

Its next claim to fame is its haunted house. After Joseph Hannath purchased the 16th century Sparrow Hall nearly 200 years ago, he renamed it Hannath Hall. He had two loves, his wife and his horse. When Mrs Hannath died he placed her open coffin in the bedroom at the northern end of the gallery on the first floor, which became known as the 'haunted' bedroom, and had meals sent up to her three times a day. At the end of six weeks he interred her under a horse chestnut tree which he planted in the front garden.

He buried his dead horse under another horse chestnut alongside the stables, which he could easily see from his window and every day an armful of hay was placed next to the animal's grave.

Strange noises have been heard from time to time in the 'haunted' room and in many parts of the house, which has attracted members of the Society for Psychical Research to visit the hall on many occasions, sometimes accompanied by representatives of the Cambridge University Society for Research in Parapsychology. Their findings and those of other researchers are documented in *Frontiers of the Unknown. The Insights of Psychical Research* by Andrew MacKenzie published by Arthur Barker Ltd.

Many apparitions have been sighted such as the one reported on the 22nd April, 1959 when the tenant's wife was sitting at the table of her sitting-room and looked towards the door of the small box-room, which she could see over her right shoulder. In the doorway was a small fair-haired boy aged between six and eight years looking round the half-opened door of that empty room, then he vanished like a ghost. Four months later at about the same time of day, she saw the same boy in the same place looking round the half-opened door. He appeared to be wearing a white frilly necked smock or nightgown and had long hair which curled at the ends.

Over the ensuing years more phenomena have been recorded at Hannath Hall, but the present tenants say that during their stay nothing untoward has happened which could not be given a practical explanation. However, this residence which stands in Hannath Road, has earned itself the reputation of being probably the best known 'haunted house' in this area.

WANDLEBURY

The Gog Magog Hills

ALTHOUGH outside the Fen Country these chalk hills, which are 300 ft at their highest point, look out over the fens and on a clear day you can see Ely Cathedral, some 20 miles away. They lie south east of Cambridge off the A1307.

According to legend they are the burial place of Gog and Magog, the last of an ancient race of giants. Mention is made in the 17th and 18th centuries of a giant, carved on the hillside at Wandlebury, possibly of prehistoric origin. A giant horse is supposed to be buried nearby and a golden chariot is hidden under Murtlow Hill.

Wandlebury Ring is an Iron Age fort which stands on the highest point of the hills and was once the stronghold of Boudicca and the Iceni. Later it became a Roman encampment and later still was ruled by a legendary warring night-rider whom nobody could defeat. All challengers were compelled to ride unaccompanied into the camp on a moonlight night and call, 'Knight to knight, come forth!' and the warrior would ride out on a jet-black charger to accept the challenge which he always won.

Sir Osbert, son of Hugh, did battle with the guardian of Wandlebury and knocked him to the ground. As he was leading the magnificent horse away the fallen warrior threw his own lance like a javelin which lodged itself in Sir Osbert's thigh. He managed to take the horse back to Cambridge, but the animal vanished the next dawn and was never seen again. Sir Osbert had a perpetual reminder of the wound sustained at Wandlebury, for on each anniversary of the fight his injury broke open and bled as if it were freshly inflicted.

WANSFORD BRIDGE

The Shepherd of Wansford Bridge

WANSFORD BRIDGE is a lost hamlet which once stood close to Mumby-cum-Chapel, which prior to 1896 comprised the two parishes now known as Mumby and Chapel St Leonards.

A legendary flood devastated the area as predicted by

the local magician, Doctor Stefan, who was blamed for all the troubles which occurred at Wansford Bridge and its neighbours.

Barnaby the shepherd always got on well with the magician, who attended his own ills and those of his animals, and he took no notice of the rumours which surrounded this strange man who walked about with a big book under his arm, muttering strange incantations. Neither did he join the large crowd which gathered to see Doctor Stefan being taken to prison on a charge of magic, this time for cursing the neighbourhood and foretelling impending floods and strange heavenly signs. He took pity on the prisoner and tried to help him escape, but it was impossible. However, Barnaby was told to remember the warning which had landed him in jail – that with the rising of the moon, in thirteen days time, a terrible storm would devastate the area. The magician told him to look after his sheep or they would be drowned. He added that when the clouds darkened and the moon appeared with a silver ring in the sky, Barnaby should drive his fattest sheep to the top of the tower, for disaster would come quickly to Wansford. He should stay with the sheep until the storm finished or else he would perish.

The shepherd was about to say goodbye when he heard drunken snores coming from the guard and took the opportunity of freeing his friend from his tiny cell. With a strange laugh Stefan disappeared and was never seen again, but his voice lingered on, 'Remember to watch for the signs of the tempest which will come thirteen days from now!' An unsuccessful search was made for the fugitive and Barnaby was never questioned.

The weather continued fine and warm and he began to doubt the wisdom of Stefan's prophecy. Then on the twelfth day the weather changed and the Wansford shepherd reminded his fellows of the magician's predictions concerning the terrible storm and suggested in vain that they take steps to save themselves and their stock.

Barnaby selected his best sheep and drove them to a fold close to the church and saw with horror the dark clouds rolling in from the west. Then the pale moon came out from behind a cloud, surrounded by a broad silver ring. It was the cunning man's prophecy and the shepherd set about his work.

As the church clock struck the last note of midnight, Barnaby, who was standing at the topmost window, saw a huge tidal wave heading straight for Wansford. He seized a bell-rope and swinging backwards and forwards with its weight, tolled his warning until he was half dead. The rain fell in torrents, the river burst its banks and its water crashed over fields, trees, barns and houses and lashed ominously at the foot of Barnaby's refuge.

The whole area was inundated with deep swirling water, imprisoning the shepherd and his flock in the tower for two days and nights, with nothing to eat or drink. However, on the third day the waters receded and he was able to float off on a make-shift raft and get fodder for his sheep, which was lowered down from the upper window of the inn, where a few lucky people were sheltering.

Scores of people and thousands of animals were drowned, but many had been saved thanks to the warning bell. Farms and homes were destroyed and even the church was ruined, except for its tower which had sheltered the best sheep in the hamlet and the heroic Shepherd of Wansford.

WELNEY

The Legend of Gold Hill

GOLD HILL is a barely visible rise, close to the One Hundred Foot river bridge and adjacent to the B1411 Welney to Littleport road. There is a small cluster of houses on this 'hill' and a dirt track leads to a public footpath. An ancient trackway linking Wisbech and Littleport is thought to have passed near this spot before the Fens were drained.

The ghost of a female robber is believed to haunt the area, searching for her share of lost gold, alleged to be part of King John's treasure, which the history books presume was lost in the sands of the Wash when he was heading north to Newark, waging war against his barons.

According to this traditional Fen story the treasure was stolen and hidden at Gold Hill, hence its name. King John had stopped off at Wisbech Castle and a local girl kept him warm that night. The next morning he awoke to find that both she, his servant and all his treasure was missing and he set off empty handed.

The girl and her servant accomplice stole two horses and made their getaway down the lonely track which led to Littleport. After several miles they were accosted by several foot-pads who pulled them from their horses. The couple were forced at knife point to open up the bags and fearing for their lives, the treasure was disclosed.

The bandits were impressed with their story and the loot and invited them to join their gang. The travellers agreed, being only too pleased to get away with their lives. For a joke the servant's livery was bundled inside two treasure bags and sent that day to King John, first by boat to Lynn and then by road to Nottinghamshire. It is said that the monarch was so angry when he received the packages at Newark Castle, that he went mad and burst a blood vessel in his brain and died.

The royal spoils were divided equally amongst the criminals, who carefully hid their shares in boxes under the floor of their hut at Gold Hill. Nine months to the night after her romp at Wisbech, the girl gave birth to a boy, whom she appropriately named 'Prince,' who grew into the finest robber in the whole of Fenland.

They had to be careful how they spent their fortune, much of which remained hidden for many years. One day a great flood drowned the robbers and washed away their hut and the treasure remained undisturbed until the Dutch drainers came in 1650 and dug the Hundred Foot Bank, which lies in front of the old mound. Gold coins glinted on their wooden mud sloughs before being hastily secreted in their foreign pockets and soon the murderous 'Fen Tigers' got word of what was happening and came in search of them and the treasure, which they claimed was theirs by right. With all the skill of their namesakes, they stalked their prey who were ruining their environment and jumped on their backs, slicing their throats with sharp knives. They took the treasure and named the mound 'Gold Hill,' and so it is today, close to the New Bedford river or Hundred Foot Drain, but the ghost has not been seen within memory.

WICKEN

Strange Happenings at Spinney Abbey Farmhouse

THE 18th century Spinney Abbey farmhouse stands off the A1123 Wicken to St Ives Road, about a mile out of the village where once a spinney of thorn trees grew. The house is built over the cellar of the chapter house of the old Spinney Abbey and is mainly constructed from materials salvaged from that building whose ruins stand nearby.

Henry Cromwell, Oliver Cromwell's fourth son and one time Lord Lieutenant of Ireland made his home at Spinney farmhouse from 1659 to 1673 and the present family are the 4th generation of Fullers to live in this delightful, secluded residence standing close to the world famous Wicken Fen, which has remained unchanged since Saxon times.

Their house has many ghostly secrets, such as the ominous gurgling sounds coming from beneath its cellar floor, constructed some 700 years ago and still looking good. In the centre is a large area which gives a hollow sound when banged. Perhaps this might have been the old entrance to the legendary tunnel linking Spinney Abbey with Denny Abbey some five miles away? When Henry VIII's men came to ransack the priory the monks were supposed to have fled to Denny along the secret tunnel, carrying most of their treasure. Unfortunately the nuns from Denny had the same idea about Spinney and they all met in the middle. In the meantime the king's men had blocked up both entrances and left the Catholics to either starve or drown, hence the gurgling, spluttering noises from the bowels of the farmhouse.

Also in the cellar is an iron grating with chains now broken away from the wall. This is where three monks were thought to have been imprisoned or maybe left to die for murdering their prior, William de Lode, on Sunday 12th May, 1403. Why they committed the crime was never established, but the three were tried and found guilty at Cambridge Castle on 20th July 1403, but were claimed by an official of the Bishop of Ely to be his clerics, taken away and never heard of again.

Robert Fuller told me that his father, Tom, who had psychic powers and saw and heard many strange phenomena, kept his pigs in a piggery which was partly built within the old priory chapel. Although the animals were happy enough elsewhere, in these quarters they always fought whenever they got close to the old part and Tom thought it may have had something to do with the murder, which is thought to have happened at that point.

Alice Bailey, nee Money, who was in the Fuller's service, well remembers Low Sunday, (the first Sunday after Easter) 1936 when six members of the household including herself heard ghostly Latin chanting in the west part of the house. The sound quietly drifted into the room, grew louder and then faded away. Someone checked to see if the radio was switched on, but it was not. Many years before this occurrence an elderly member of the family had heard similar chanting in the stackyard, coming from the direction of the strange piggery.

I am also told that when the north wall of the house was under-pinned in 1935 a number of skeletons were found under the foundations, three of which were buried in an extremely confined space, face downwards with their legs and feet close to their skulls and it appeared that the largest body, perhaps that of a man aged 19 years old, had received a broken skull before death. It was traditional to bury 'evil' people face downwards to prevent their spirits wandering and causing trouble. The other bodies were buried correctly, but when the builders came to excavate the east side they found a large skeleton under the dining room floor. They removed its legs to make room for the concrete and the rest remains under the dining table.

Strange things still happen for in December 1991 Mr and Mrs Fuller heard the incredibly loud sound of horses' hooves in the dead of night coming from under their bedroom window, although there was no subsequent evidence to support the noise. Neither mentioned it to the other, thinking each must have been dreaming, but when Robert mentioned it to Valerie a couple of weeks later they were both flabbergasted yet unperturbed, even though Elias Fuller had heard similar sounds on several occasions in the 19th century which he believed presaged bad-luck.

The house is open to the public for bed and breakfast and despite its ghostly record is a warm, friendly farmhouse made even more cheerful by the huge log fire which blazes in the drawing room on cold nights.

WILLINGHAM

Few's Mice

THIS is now a large village off the B1050, ideal for commuting to Huntingdon and Cambridge, but when it was a small isolated community, Jabez Few, who died in the late 1920s, kept some white mice and played tricks with them. The villagers called them his imps or familiars and one day he is said to have put one in a woman's bedroom and she could not get it out. Her landlord shut a big tom cat in the room and a noisy fight ensued. Upon investigation the cat was running up and down the curtains and great clumps of fur were lying on the floor, but still the mouse could not be caught.

The landlord, Mr Dudley, was then advised to perform a spell-breaking hex which involved boiling the clippings of a horse's hoof and the legs of a toad in a stone jar over the fire. He swore and cussed at Jabez as he prepared the mixture and before he was finished Few strode into the house, whistled up his mouse and it came to him at once.

When he died his house stood empty for many years and his successor was only able to get rid of the mice by standing in running water with them, when they ran away forever.

WISBECH

The Ghost of the 'Bowling Green Tap'

IN 1965 Dick and Edna Dedman became landlords of the pleasant little Chase Street pub. For many years Edna dismissed the strange sounds which she often heard when alone as being imaginary. She did not meet the ghost cum poltergeist whom she nick-named 'Charlie,' until a few years later.

Mrs Dedman does not drink alcohol, which is the most likely reason most people would give for a landlady seeing ghosts!

It was after closing time and the Dedmans were sitting in front of the fire in the sitting room, Dick sleeping and Edna knitting. Sounds were heard coming from the locked bar across the hallway, and Edna went to investigate without disturbing her husband. For some reason she glanced to her right towards the staircase door which was shut tight and saw through it and up the dark stairs. Then as plainly as if they were bathed in spot lights, she witnessed a man slowly and silently descending the stairs, dragging an old black coffin. Edna describes him as being 'Just like the man off the Quaker Oats packet,' but this was no porridge advert; it had to be a ghost and they stared at each other.

A slight mist swirled about he who was to become 'Charlie' dressed in Quaker-style clothing, with a large, clean shaven face, and very deep-set unblinking eyes. After a few seconds, which seemed like ages, he continued his noiseless journey to the bottom of the stairs, drifted through the closed door and with difficulty manoeuvred his coffin around the end of the staircase.

Edna had to squash herself against the wall to allow him passage, but he did not acknowledge her; he walked on in his misty fashion, and stopped a few feet from the back door. The handle wizzed round and round, the chain dropped and the figure walked through the still closed door into the back yard.

After a short time Edna regained her composure and returned to the sitting room, deciding not to say a word because she knew Dick would not believe her. However, she looked so pale that he remarked that she looked awful and had she seen a ghost!

She kept her secret for a long time, but 'Charlie' was now quite active, scaring people who slept in the spare back bedroom and appearing when she was alone. One visiting niece screamed out in the night that a horrid man in an old fashioned wide-brimmed hat had tried to strangle her and she never stayed at the 'Tap' again. So much happened that in the end 'Charlie' was no longer a secret.

He once tried to pull Edna out of her chair when she was dozing in front of the fire in the bar one night and she almost ended up on the floor. Despite the glowing embers and the number of customers who had not long vacated the bar, the room felt extremely cold, the sort of temperature which puts ice on the inside of windows. On another occasion when she was crossing the ground floor hallway she heard a voice coming from the stairs which said, 'Here she comes,' and she was alone in the house.

Sometimes the ghost is not seen for a few weeks and a poltergeist, which could be 'Charlie' in disguise, takes over. Customers see bottles jump silently from top shelves onto the floor, crates of bottles jangle as if being violently shaken, door handles turn when there is nobody to turn them and things fall from walls. In the early part of 1992 a pile of torn-off raffle tickets placed on a shelf suddenly blew all over the bar, although there was no draught and the draw prize, a large toy dog, jumped off the bar and frightened most people half to death. A few weeks later customers saw and heard a large picture and two brass plates fall off the wall at the same time as the curtains and their rail crashed to the floor.

Mrs Dedman lives reasonably happily with 'Charlie' although she would never spend a night alone at the 'Tap.' She says that she actually feels it is a privilege to know him and when he gets bothersome she tells him to keep quiet or go away and he usually obeys.

WOODSTON

The Lady in Black

WOODSTON lies to the south of Peterborough and in 1908 there were reports of people walking the path near the churchyard at night seeing 'The Lady in Black,' flitting among the tombs and gravestones, as if searching for something.

According to a press report the first woman to see her fainted with shock and soon there were many ghoulish sightseers hoping to catch a glimpse of the dark spectre. Bold young men came armed with sticks determined to 'lay her ghost once and for all,' yet those who saw her rarely returned for a second look.

No one could say for sure who she was, but it was thought that she was connected with another tale circulating Woodston at that time. This was about a certain mother who was frightened that her children would not be well cared for when she died and swore on her deathbed that she would return from her grave to watch over her large family. The family is said to have lived in the Klondyke, which is now Belsize Avenue, Woodston.

In 1973 a neighbour then aged 93 told the *Peterborough Citizen & Advertiser*, 'I don't believe in ghosts and didn't take much notice of the tales I heard. But I remember hearing a few weeks after the woman died that she had been seen by her children.' More local residents who remembered the dying woman's words with horror, swore they heard strange noises coming from the house where she had lived. Her children were questioned and said they had seen their mother come back from her grave.

The old lady continued, 'The children, poor little mites that they were, often used to say their mother was with them when they crossed the road and went out alone. They had to be moved from the house in the end.'

In order to restore order to Woodston, which was now a tourist area, the local authority is said to have posted notices near the graveyard warning people to 'Beware of the ghost of the Lady in Black,' who haunted for just one year.

WROOT

Billy Lindholme

ON private land at OS SE112 713036 and adjacent to the farm track leading off the centre of the village, is a huge stone weighing perhaps half a ton. This boulder is said to have been thrown from Lindholme many hundreds of years ago by a young boy who turned into a hermit giant cum wizard and was in league with the devil.

The legendary William of Lindholme, better known as 'Billy Lindholme,' lived some 3 miles away at Lindholme on the Hatfield Moors. In later life his home was a small hermitage, supposedly on the site of the privately owned Lindholme Hall at Hatfield.

Billy's skills first came to light when he was a child and left at home to scare birds whilst his parents went off to the feast at Wroot. He was so angry that he lifted this giant stone and hurled it at the house some 3 miles distant which his parents were visiting. Fortunately it just missed its target.

The boy then went to Wroot, expecting to find his parents squashed under his missile, but all being well, mitigated his presence by assuring them that all the sparrows were safely shut up in the barn. When his mother and father returned to Lindholme they found most of the birds were dead, except for one or two, which had turned snow-white. Such a species of bird is said to have been seen in the Lindholme area as late as the end of the last century.

The farmer had to harness six strong horses to move the boulder, but the task was too strenuous and the animals died from over-exertion. The stone was rumoured to be cursed and soon it was agreed that it should remain undisturbed for all time. Its sinister powers were further embellished with the belief that if it became 'grassed over' the earth would be red with blood. I am told that in about 1976 it was moved and within two years the person responsible suffered a tragic bereavement in his family. Some people did wonder if there was a connection between the two happenings.

Standing on private land close to Lindholme Hall is the 'Little Finger Stone' which is quite large and has an indentation supposedly made by the little finger. About a mile away and still inaccessible to the general public is the 'Thumb Stone' which is reputed to bring bad luck if it is moved and has a 'thumb' mark on it. All these stones are probably an example of our need to rationalize the extraordinary, and large stones are very rare in peat land.

'Billy Lindholme's' great strength became well known and on one occasion he was able to rope a whole haystack onto his back and take it home for his cattle and to make a mattress.

A legendary unfinished causeway, said to be Billy's handiwork, led from Hatfield Moor to Wroot. This is on private land commencing at approximately OS SE112 710056, but has been obliterated by peat digging. He undertook to do the work as fast as a man could gallop a horse, on condition that the rider should not look behind him. The man had not travelled far when he heard such a terrible commotion that he was compelled to turn round. To his horror he saw gravel and stones hurtling about in all directions, with the giant in the middle accompanied by hundreds of little demons dressed in red jackets laying cobbles as fast as they could go.

The terrified horseman exclaimed, 'God speed your work,' which put a stop to the undertaking and left the people who had to travel between Lindholme and Hatfield to wade through the bog for another two hundred years.

Billy was said to be able to foretell the time of his own death and when it was close he dug a grave over which a huge flag stone was supported by a stout pole. Billy Lindholme lay down in the hole, removed the prop and buried himself alive.

LINCOLNSHIRE DIALECT

Albins	Unable, maybe
Abraid	Similar
Addle	To earn
Addlins	Wages
Agait	Doing or starting something
Ager	The ague
Aist	Are you?
Alegar	Vinegar made out of beer
All-a-bits	All in pieces
All-along	Because of
All-to-nowt	All gone
Anshum-scranshum	Topsy-turvy, disorderly
Arsy-varsy	Vice-versa, wrong way round
Ask	Sour or dry tasting
At-nowt	On no account
Attramite	A dirty child
Aud-farrand	Old fashioned, out of date
Awm	To loll about
Back-end	The latter end of the year
Bag-a-Moonshine	A yarn or foolish tale
Baggerment	Rubbish, silly talk
Bantling	A small child
Barf	Isolated or detached hill
Barnacles	A pair of spectacles
Battle-twig	Earwig
Beale	The lowing of cattle, to cry out
Beeson/beezen	Blind
Beffling	Coughing or barking
Belder	To roar or cry
Belker	Huge
Belly-wark	The colic or stomach ache
Benzil	To beat well
Besslings	First milk of a newly calved cow
Bezzle	To gulp one's drink
Bile	A boil
Binjer	An advanced state of drunkenness
Blackey	A blackbird
Blacksmith's Daughter	A padlock
Blash	Nonsense
Blashey	Thin or watery
Blashing	Flourishing, extensive

Bleb	A blister or bubble
Blocker	Very drunk
Blossam	A scruffy girl
Blunt	Cash
Bluther-bunged	To lose the thread when speaking
Bocken	To be scared
Bogle	A goblin often found in wetlands
Boggart	A goblin
Bogs-me-Rolly	A threat to chastise
Boke	About to vomit
Bone	To steal
Bossacks	A fat, lazy woman
Bottle	A bundle
Boykin	A small boy
Brades-o-me	Similar to me
Brangle	To dispute, to mix up
Braunge	To strut about
Breeder	A boil
Breedlings	Fen dwellers
Broggle	To poke
Broodle	To cherish or fondle
Brook	A boil or abcess
Brown Titus	Bronchitus
Buck-stick	An old friend or old fashioned man or boy
Bundle-off	To dismiss
Bunts	Half corn and half chaff
Butty	A friend, a mate
Ca-craw	A carrion crow
Caffle	To prevaricate
Cagmags	Inferior
Capper	A superior article or puzzling thing
Casson	Cow dung dried for fuel
Cat-blash	Worthless drink or a weak argument
Cat-haw	Hawthorn berry
Cautionable	Incautious
Caw	Short of breath
Cazzlety	Unsettled
Chappy	Impertinent
Chark	To line a well with bricks
Charmed	Eaten by rats or mice
Chat	The chaffinch
Chattle	To chat
Chelp	Impertinence
Chep	To be saucy or cheeky

106

Cheps	The face
Chess	To crack
Chowsle	To chew
Chumpy	Short or thick
Clags	Dirty wool clipped from sheep
Clammed	Grasped or seized
Clanch	To snatch rudely and violently
Clarrip	To strike a hearty blow
Clat	To bedaub
Clatty	Sticky or dirty
Clazum	Force, violence
Clink	Smart
Clinker	Superior, immense
Clink-and-clean	Well completed or done
Clipper	A good one
Clipping	Very good
Clishawk	To steal
Clook	To steal
Closens	Fields
Cloudations	An abundance of anything
Clubtail	A stoat
Clumpsed	Cold, benumbed
Clunch	Sullen or stiff clay
Clung	Heavy soil
Coath	To faint
Cock-apparel	Pomp or great pride in a little matter
Cockling	Tottery
Cocket	Getting better after an illness
Cod	To deceive
Coitey	Dangling an infant
Coney-fogle	To cheat
Conny	Nice, pretty
Cosher	A huge thing
Cow-cumber	Cucumber
Cow-lady	Ladybird
Cramble	To walk stiffly
Crawk	The core of fruit, the heart of a haystack
Cree	To boil gently over the fire
Cronno	Correct
Croodle	To sit or lie together for warmth
Crowner	Extremely good
Crowner's-quest	Coroner's inquest
Cruds	Curds

Dabchick	A moor hen
Dacker	To slow down
Daisy-me!	An exclamation of surprise
Darklings	Twilight
Daul	To weary
Dead-herse	To receive payment in advance
Dead-nailer	Something astonishing
Dilly	Vehicle for removing night soil
Ding	A blow or a thump
Doggerybaw	Nonsense
Don	Clever
Door-darn	Door-post
Dot-and-go-one	A lame person
Dowter	Daughter
Dubbs	Two
Dulbert	Dull or stupid
Dung	To impart knowledge
Eadily	Insufficient
Earnings	Rennet used for cheese making
East	Yeast
East-punkit	Wooden vessel to hold yeast
Elted-up	Bedaubed with mud
End	To spoil or destroy
Enew	Enough, sufficient
Enow	Shortly, presently
Ewst	Used, was accustomed to
Ewt	Owed
Fast-nas-Tuesday	Shrove Tuesday
Fat-shag	Bacon
Feat	Neat
Feeting	Footprints
Fezzon-penny	Money spent on a bargain
Fick-fack	To waste time
Fid-Fad	To poke your nose in where it is not wanted
Flam	A falsehood told in jest
Flather	Ridiculous conversation
Flim-flam	A trick, a whim
Flimsy	Ill-tempered
Fluther-gullion	One who has much to say about nothing
Fluter	A blow
Fogo	A nasty smell
Fond	Foolish, dim-witted
Fowty	Fusty or tainted

Frangy	Spirited or lively
Fruggans	A slovenly woman
Fummard	A pole cat
Funkey	Nervous, frightened
Gallus	Mischievous, sly
Gallontee	Guarantee
Galloses	Braces to hold up trousers
Gath	Homestead, farm
Garth	Safe enclosed land for cattle
Gate	Ways, habits
Gawm	To stare vacantly
Gaw-maw	A staring vacant person
Gawster	To laugh loudly
Gessling	A gosling
Gifts	White spots on the finger nails
Gingham	Umbrella
Gizzen	To stare vacantly
Gleg	To give someone a sly look
Glib	Slippery
Glur	Very fat bacon
Glyster	To chastise, to correct
Gnag	To gnaw like a rat or mouse
Gomeril	A stupid person
Gotes	Outfalls, sluices for draining the land
Goy!	An exclamation instead of swearing
Grains	The fangs of a tooth
Grobble	To grope
Grock	Anything stunted in growth
Growse	To eat noisely
Gykes	Way, method
Gyle holes	Shallows or backwaters left by the tide
Hackering	Stuttering or stammering
Habited	Accustomed
Haking	Idling about
Hame	Steam from boiling water
Hamagagged	Pleased
Hanchum-scranshum	Scarcity of food
Hap-up	To wrap up, to cover up
Happing	Wrapping, night clothing
Harden-faced	Impertinent
Hardlins	Hardly, scarcely
Hard-set	In a difficult position
Hard-lines	Severe terms

Harr	A sea mist
Haw-buck	A vulgar country lout
Hawm	To lounge about
Hazing	A beating
Heder	A male lamb
Heft	The handle of anything
Herrin-saw	A heron
Hessle	A beating or thrashing
Hinder-ends	Refuse of any grain
Hipe	To walk lamely
Hister	To be off, disperse
Hivy-skivy	In utter confusion
Hobby-herse	The dragon fly
Hobnail	A loutish rustic
Hockle	To walk lamely
Hockerdols	The feet
Hog	A young sheep
Hooker	Immense
Hornery	Anything ordinary or inferior
Hossuk	To laugh loudly
Howlt	Small plantation of trees
Hut	The finger of a glove used to cover a wounded finger
Huzzing	A whirring noise
Ings	Open meadows
Inkle	Gramatical
Ither	The udder of a cow or goat
Ivey-skivy	To make an uproar
Izerum	A tedious yarn
Izles	Floating particles of soot
Jacketing	A bleating
Jangle	To wrangle
Jannack	Satisfactory, pleasant, just
Jazzen	A donkey
Jemmy	A sheep's head
Jerry's	The south, used with reference to the direction of the wind
Jew's-trump	The Jew's harp
Jiffling	To fidget
Jiggard	Surprised
Jiste	To take in another person's cattle to graze
Jorum	A large quantity
Joss	To pay or treat

110

Joskin	A raw country lad
Jowt	To shake
Judy	A female of curious appearance
Jugging	A lot of rain
Jumblement	Confusion
Jumpers	Maggots
Junk	A lump
Kades	Animals reared by artificial feeding
Keb	To sob and pant for breath
Kebbing	To shake with sobbing
Kedge	To fill or stuff
Kedge-bellied	Remark concerning the fat belly of a greedy person
Kelcher	A large one
Kelter	Rubbish
Kelterment	Rubbish
Kelps	An awkward fellow
Kens-speck	Easy to recognise
Kevassing	Running about
Kibunkus	Bronchitus
Kid	A faggot or bundle of sticks
Kimnelles	A shallow tub, about 6″ deep to work butter in
Kittling	A kitten
Knag	To gnaw
Koakum	To out-wit a person
Lace	To flog
Lagged	Very tired
Laking-about	Wasting time
Lalder	To sing loudly and out of key
Lall	To stick out one's tongue
Lallup	To beat or flog
Lap	To fold
Lap-up	To inter
Lap-eared	Large eared
Lape	To walk through mud
Lapping up	End, conclusion
Larum	A worthless tale
Larrup	To beat or flog
Lasher	Large
Laumpus	An idler
Let-in	Deceived
Lig	To lie down
Lillylow	Hot, bright flame

Limmack	Pliable
Limbo	A gaol
Lob-scrooge	Porridge
Lobbing	Bending from own weight
Lodlum	Laudanum
Lollaker	The tongue
Looby	A coward
Lop	A flea
Loppard	Sour milk
Lubbard	A blockhead
Lunch	The sound made by the fall of a heavy but yielding body
Lungeous	Rough and rude
Manafogal	To invent
Manner	Manure
Martin	A twin female calf
Marvels	Marbles
Mash	To throw about
Masher	Large
Mattler	One of a pair, equal
Maul	To fatigue
Mawks	Maggots
Mawkin	Scarecrow, silly fellow
Mawps	A slow, silly person
Mawping	Walking idly
Maze	To amaze
Mazzle	To confuse
Mazzarded	Stunned, amazed
Meagrim	Headache
Meagrims	Tricks
Messengers	Dark patches of cloud
Minch	To mince
Moak	Fog
Moastlings	Frequently
Mold	Earth, soil
Mullakin	Toiling hard
Nang-nail	A corn or bunion
Nappers	The knees
Nawp	A blow usually to the side of the head
Nawpy	Shrewd, clever
Near	Mean, stingy
Neb	The bill of a bird
New-ber	A cow which has recently calved

Noddy	A fool who nods when he should speak
Nointer	Large
Nookings	The bottom corner of a sack or bag
Nosker	Large
Nunty	Small in stature, neat and precise in dress
Nye	Near, stingy, mean
Oddling	One differing from the rest
Orts	Wasteful, leaving of food
Outners	Strangers
Ovened	Wind on the stomach
Owd-hunks	A mean person
Owery	Damp, cold, filthy
Pad	A footpath
Pag	To carry on the back
Pannikin	Confusion, uproar
Par	Hencoop
Parement	To speak harm of someone
Pash	Rottenness
Pawps	An ignorant or slow person
Pawt	The hand
Penny	Covered with young feathers
Piltripely	Anything mean or indifferent
Plait	To entangle
Plugger	Large
Polly-cot	A man who does housework
Pot-noddle	Tadpole
Prog	Food, victuals
Pronkus	A donkey
Pulk	A coward
Purr	The fire poker
Pyewipe	Peewit
Quick-sticks	Immediately
Quidder	A horse which chews its food into lumps and then spits it out
Quift	Trick, unusual method
Quilt	To strike
Quitter	An unhealthy pussy growth on a horse's foot
Raave-up	To bring up old grievances
Rack-a-pelt	A riotous noisy fellow
Raffle	To confuse

113

Rafty	Rancid
Ralakin-rooser	Extremely large
Rammel	Hard rubbish such as broken bricks
Ramper	The highway
Rawm	To shout loudly
Reasty	Rancid, especially bacon
Reckling	The smallest pig in the litter
Remble	To move
Rightle	To put in order
Rightle-comb	A pocket comb
Rip	A tramp
Roaky	Misty, foggy
Sawmpy	Feeble-minded
Sawney	A simpleton
Scafe	A mean person
Scanny	Mean
Scrat	To barely make a living, to scratch
Sea-harr	Sea mist
Sea-maw	Seagull
Seg	Old boar pig
Shack-bags	Idle tramp
Shammacks	The legs
Sheeder	A female animal
Shucky	Mean and shifty
Signhills	The sea bank
Sky-wannock	On the side, sideways
Slumpton	An untidy person
Smopple	Weak or brittle
Snag	Luncheon
Sparrow-gress	Asparagus
Spane	To wean a child
Spang	To throw down or shut violently
Splauts	The feet
Sprunny	A sweetheart or lover
Strap	Credit
Strunchion	A long tale or story
Sturky	Short or undersized
Swabby	A person who is either fat or short
Take no payment	No harm will come to that thing
Tem	To unload
Tent	To look after or watch over
Tharms	Intestines of a small pig
Thick-wet	Saturated with water

114

Thribbs	Three
Thruffing	The whole matter
Thusking	Very large
Tiddy	Small
Tilly-willie	Very small
Tit	A favourite horse
Todlowries	The undead
Tommy	Bread
Tom-tawdry	Cheap finery
Trash-bags	A worthless person
Trig	Precise, neat
Tumpoke	To turn head over heels
Tut	A ghost
Uncoomed	Not arrived
Undid	Undone
Unheppen	Clumsy, unskilful
Unpossible	Impossible
Unsneck	Unfasten
Uvvers	Rough grass
Vaals	Presents given to servants
Vangalized	Galvanized
Wacker	Very large
Waffy	Silly, weak minded
Wankle	A weak child
Watter-jawled	Land covered with water
Waxey	Annoyed
Welker	A big size
Weney	In bad health
Werrit	To tease or fidget
Wong	Low lying land
Wottle-days	Week days
Wykings	The corners of the mouth
Yanks	Gaiters
Yarker	Large
Yawnups	An ignorant person
Yother	To eat greedily
Yuvling	A whisp of straw

115

DIALECT OF THE FEN COUNTRY

Addle	To grow, to thrive
Agist	Take in and look after cattle
Arsle	To fidget
About in your dissables	Wearing your old clothes
Beaver boots	Heavy duty leather ankle boots
Beastings/Beslings/	
Bislings	First milk taken from newly calved cow
Bishy-barnabee	Ladybird
Blar	Cry
Blee	Waterlogged
Bor	Young man or boy
Bottle	A bundle of straw or hay
Botty	Over particular, fussy
Boykin	A boy
Brangle	Dispute or quarrel
Breed	Once through a field with a plough
Brights	Brass ornaments
Budget	Leather shoulder bag contining tools etc.
Bulls Noon	A long time hence or never
Bungo	Cheese
Buskins	Leather gaiters
Cady	An animal which has become less boisterous
Cag mag	Course, inferior or bad meat
Chambled	Eaten by rats or mice
Chelpy-cheppy	Saucy
Chip-out	A quarrel
Chummie	A woollen hat which pulls over the ears, often has a pom-pom on top
Clags	Dirty wool clipped off sheep
Claggy	Sticky
Clamp	Root crop storage heap covered with straw and earth
Clammed	Parched with thirst
Clarty	Bedaubed in sugar or syrup
Clat	A tell-tale
Clatty	Sticky
Clout	A dish-cloth

116

Clow or clough	A flood-gate, the gates of a sluice
Clunch	Blunt, short-tempered
Come to mine	Visit my house
Come to yours	I will visit your house
Combe of corn	18 stones
Coppling	Unsteady from being top-heavy
Corned	Worse the wear for drink, 'market-merry!'
Cow lady	Ladybird
Craze	To pester or annoy
Cramble	To hobble
Cree	To boil gently
Crone	An old toothless sheep
Cuffing a parle	Gossiping
Dackering	Slowing down
Daggerly	Damp
Dickey	A donkey
Ding	A blow to the head, ear etc.
Dockey	Meal break taken in the fields at 10.00 or 11.00 am
Doughty	A one horned beast, goat etc.
Drizzled up	Wrinkled
Dringle	To be lazy or slow
Dubbed	Cut off
Dudder	Shiver
Dullerin'	A noise in the head
Dwoile	A floor cloth
Dythes	Cow-dung tempered and prepared for burning
Earnest	Money given to confirm a contract, or a hiring between master and servant, given especially at Hiring Fairs
Eau	Water, a drain
Eddish	First growth of grass after mowing
Eldern	The elder tree
Elbows out	Impoverished
Eshbuck	A false link, used in temporary repairs of chains
Enew	Enough
Ever-readies/	
Free traders/	All names for split legged knickers, joined at the
Split arsed mechanics	waistband and fastened with tape
Fairish on	Steady progress
Far	To happen, either well or ill
Felfer	Sometimes, felt

Fell	Fierce
Fellon	A whitlow
Fen Nightingales	Frogs
Fending and Proving	Arguing
Fezzon	To fasten
Fleak	Hunk of straw cut from stack
Fleak knife	Knife used for above purpose
Fliggers	Reeds growing by edge of river or dyke
Flimiticate	Effect genteel manners
Flimmock	Fussy
Flit	Move about, remove household goods
Foursies	Break for tea in fields at 4.00 pm
Footy	Small, usually in bad sense
Frame about	Have affected mannerisms
Franks	Herons
Frawn	Frozen
Frezed	A person is frozen, 'Frezed from head to toe!'
Frit	Past tense of frightened, 'He frit me!'
Fussy	Delighted
Gallus	Mischievous, sly
Gansey	Sleeveless pullover
Gathered finger	A pussy finger
Gauby	A lout
Gays	Pictures
Gays (Looking at)	Looking at a picture book
Get wrong	Be told off, 'You'll get wrong by your mum if you do that!'
Get about	To become convalescent after an illness
Gifts	White specks on the finger nails
Girn	To grin
Gollop	Eat quickly
Gote	A watercourse, outlet of a drain
Goudle	To flog
Gnag	To gnaw
Grunt	Nonsense, 'He talks a load a' grunt!'
Gulsh	Corpulent, short and thick
Ha	Not straight, 'cut on the ha' or 'the ha side of the road'
Hack and splutter	Stammer
Harnsers	Herons
Hawbuck	A raw country lad
Hedge mumper	A tramp
Hedgeups	Sparrows

118

Hedgerow inspector	A tramp
Hen's noseful	A small quantity
Hernshaw/Herringshaw/	
Heronshaws	Herons
Higgle	To haggle
Higgler	A man who keeps horses and works them for hire
Hive off	To reprimand
Hodmedod/hodendod/	
Hodnydod	The snail
Hodnydods	Rags used for curling the hair, so called as when in place the prepared hair resembled snails
Hog	A lamb aged from six months until first shorn
Ho-go	A vile smell
Holt	Plantation, especially of willows
Hulk	Slit and de-gut a rabbit or hare
Hunny	To fondle
Hutkin	Finger stall to cover wound
Ill-thriven	A delicate, poorly nurtured person
Imbrangled	Mixed-up, confused
Ings	Low lying grass lands and meadows
Inner girl	The house maid in a farm-house
Inquiration	An enquiry
Jack-on-the-pinch	A make-shift job
Jack-straw	The man who used to carry the straw from the threshing-machine to the straw stacks. Also applied to the straw elevator
Jarzen	A donkey. A 'boozin' jarzen' is a drinking, or drunken lout
Jemmy	A sheep's head or something neat and smart
Jobber	A dealer in livestock
Joey	Long round tube for keeping sack neck open
Johnny Moblin's	Poor results from an under-manned gang
Joskin	A raw youth
Kaffle	To prevaricate
Karke	Care, worry. Also sickness or rejection of food with nausea
Keeping room	The room usually occupied by the family
Kell	The inner or loose fat of a pig
Kelter	Nonsense, rubbish, household knick-knacks. Also slang word for money
Kids	Long bundles of thorns tied with three bands, used for fencing around or between crew yards

Kittle	'The cat has kittled' — she has given birth
Knag	To gnaw
Knanging	Grumbling, discontented
Lad's love	Name for the Southern-wood plant, used to attract females
Laid corn	Corn flattened by wind and rain
Lallygags	Leather straps worn over trousers from ankles to knees to stop rats running up legs
Lap	Thin broth or porridge
Lape	To walk carelessly in the dirt
Last	A last of corn = ten quarters
Leam/Lode	A drainage channel
Longtails	Pheasants
Loppered	Milk turned sour or coagulated
Lor bor s'imme	Expression such as 'Good gracious me!'
Lummox	Clumsy person
Mallyrag	To cut or carve awkwardly
Management	Chemical or artificial manure
Mawkin	Scare-crow
Mawther	Young girl
May-hap	Perhaps
Mizzy/mozzy	Confused, bewildered, dazed
Mog	To move on
Moon	Yard lamp
Mort	A considerable number
Mure-hearted	Too kind hearted for one's own good
'Nation/'nationly	Very, exceedingly
Nappers	Knees
Natter	To find fault in a nasty way
Natteral	A kind, simple, foolish person
Near	Mean, stingy, penurious
Neck or nothing	Ready to run all hazards
New-beared	Applied to cow that has recently calved
Nine-corns	Small pipe of tobacco, 'You've just time for nine corns more!'
Nobby	A foal
'Noll'	Fen nickname for Oliver Cromwell
No nation place	A lonely, out-of-the-way, lawless place
Ochre	Money, especially gold
Ocksecrotia	Tipsy

Odd	Alone, lonely
Odd-cum-shorts	Oddments, fragments
Odling	Without equal
Ol' boy	A young man
Old woman's luck	To have the wind in the face on journey out and back as well
Orts	Wasteful leavings of food
Outner	A stranger
Owry/owley	Dirty, filthy
Pad the hoof	To travel on foot
Paigle	Cowslip
Pammy	A thick, soft, fleshy hand was called a 'pammy' hand
Parl	Conversation
Pash	Any decayed or rotten substance
Pattens	An iron ring screwed to shoes to lift feet above mud or water level. Also Fen word for skates, sometimes called 'Ice-pattens.'
Pay one's moon dues	To be a bit 'soft in the head.'
Pie/pye	A small round stack of mustard
Pig-cheer	Pork-pies, sausages etc., the proceeds of pig-killing
Pikey	Derisory name for a gypsy
Pinfold	An animal pound
Pink	The chaffinch
Pingle	Small enclosure of low shrubs or underwood or gorse
Pingle	To eat with little or no appetite. 'He is a pingling feeder.'
Plash	To lay a hedge
Plash	Low wet land
Pluck a crow	To pick a quarrel
Plumpendicular	Perpendicular
Pock-arred	Pock-marked from the small pox
Polly-coddle	An effeminate man or boy
Potchap	Inferior crockery
Potlicka	Vegetable liquor left in saucepan
Puckaterry	To be in a muddle
Pulk	A coward
Purl	A small stream
Push	A pimple
Quality	The gentry
Quick sticks	Immediately

Quilt	To beat
Quizzy	Nosey
Rack-a-pelt	An idle troublesome vagabond
Rack up	The last food given to horses at night
Raff	A scab
Raffle	To confuse
Rafty	Fusty, rancid
Rammil	Broken bricks, rubbish, burnt clay
Ramper	A raised road which protected lands from floods
Randy	A drinking bout
Ranny	The field mouse or shrew
Rarely	Uncommonly well
Rave up	To repeat old stories
Reasty	Rancid, applied to bacon. Also restive
Reckling	The weakest pig of a litter, anything weak or deformed
Remble	To remove or change places
Rightle	Put to rights
Rightling comb	A pocket comb for the hair
Roak	A thick mist or haze
Rommocking	Romping, as a boisterous cow
Rone	The roe of a fish
Ruck	A crowd
Runty	Ill-tempered
Sad-bad	Extremely bad
Save-all	A stingy or mean fellow
Scour	To cleanse out and deepen a dyke
Scradge/cradge	To raise and strengthen a bank with clay
Scrat	To scratch. To make a living with difficulty
Scrawmy	Tall, awkward, ungainly, applied to people and crops
Scroof	Rubbish
Shackles	Broth made from a sheep's head
Shock	Group of corn sheaves stood up in fields
Shining eyes	Much relished globules of fat floating on top of gravy
Shove	A sheaf of corn
Shut knife	A pocket knife
Sidle	Sideways
Slacker	A small sluice for regulating the flow of water by means of a sliding door
Slabber	Foam at the mouth

122

Slathe	(To rhyme with 'carve.') To Smear. 'He slathed his hands down the wall.'
Slap	To spill
Slod	Wade through mud
Slodgers	Fen folk who walked through the wetlands on stilts and jumped dykes using a leaping pole
Slop	A smock frock. A loose over-garment made of thick cotton or linen.
Slough	(Rhymes with 'rough') a wooden shovel for casting out mud from Fen drains
Slub	Mud
Slugger	A black eye, a heavy blow
Slummocky	Untidy
Smack	A taste, a small quantity
Smeeth	(Pronounced 'Smee') A level plain as in 'Marshland Smeeth.'
Smur	A drizzle — smur of rain
Sosh	Lop-sided — the sosh side of the road
Spit brown	Chewing tobacco
Squit	Rubbish – also to talk a lot of nonsense
Toadman	A horseman who had sold his soul to the devil using a natter-jack toad in return for complete mastery over his horses
Tossled	Tangles
Tract	Good natured
Trandling	Trapping birds and rabbits etc at night by two people dragging a net over the stubble fields
Tret	Past tense of treat
Tudded	Bewitched
'Wag'	Nickname for anyone called Charles
Weather breeder	Unusually fine weather which gives false hopes that unseasonally warm weather is to follow.
Whaddon organs	Frogs
Whelm	To turn something upside down
Wheret	An annoying person
Winnol Weather	Stormy weather at the beginning of March which usually coincides with the Winnald Fair held at Downham Market, Norfolk
Wittery	Weak
Wurritz	An annoying child
Yorks	See 'Lallygags'

BIBLIOGRAPHY

An Historical Account of Wisbech William Watson 1827
The Fenland Story W E Dring FLA, Cambridgeshire Libraries 1967
The Folklore Society County Folklore Series No. V, Folklore Concerning Lincolnshire, Gutch & Peacock 1908
Legends & Traditions of Huntingdonshire W H B Saunders, Simpkin Marshall & Co 1913
Croyland Abbey Official Guide
Lincolnshire Folklore Ethel H Rudkin 1936
Epworth, the home of the Wesleys W Le Cato Edwards
Fenland Saints Shrines and Churches Written and published by Trevor Bevis
The Companion Guide to East Anglia John Seymour, Collins
Folk Heroes of Britain Charles Kightly, Thames and Hudson
Legends and Traditions of Huntingdonshire W H B Saunders, Simpkin Marshall & Co 1913
Cambridgeshire Customs and Folklore Edith Porter, Routledge & Kegan Paul
Hero Myths & Legends of the British Race M I Ebbutt MA, George G Harrap & Co 1910
By-Gone Lincolnshire Ed. W Andrews FRHS, A Brown & Sons 1891
A Glossary or Collection of Words, Phrases, Place Names, Superstitions etc Current in East Lincolnshire Written and published by Jabez Good
Tales from the Fens W H Barrett, Routledge & Kegan Paul
More Tales from the Fens W H Barrett, Routledge & Kegan Paul
Folk-Lore, Vol 11 June 1891 No. 11 The Folklore Society
Stamford Myths & Legends Martin Smith, Paul Watkins, Stamford
Stories from Doddington Hall Printed by F W Cupit (Printers) Ltd, Horncastle, Lincs
The Exning Story Compiled by Roy Tricker, The Parochial Church Council of Exning and West Landwade
Frontiers of the Unknown. The Insights of Psychical Research Andrew Mackenzie, Arthur Barker Ltd
Spinney Abbey, Wicken Michael Rouse
Gazeteer of British Ghosts Peter Underwood, Souvenir Press
Fenland Notes and Queries
Lincolnshire Notes and Queries

Index